OVERCOMING TRIALS WITH TRUST

A Single Mother's Journey

I0540019

Kyianne Joy Harewood

Copyright © 2025 by Kyianne Joy Harewood

All rights reserved. No part of this publication may be reproduced, distributed, or transmitted in any form or by any means, including, photocopying,recording, or other electronic or mechanical methods, without the prior written permission of the copyright owner and the publisher, except in the case of brief quotations embodied in critical reviews and certain other noncommercial uses permitted by copyright law. For permission requests, write to the publisher, addressed "Attention: Permissions Coordinator," at the address below.

ARPress
45 Dan Road Suite 15
Canton MA 02021
Hotline: 1(888) 821-0229
Fax: 1(508) 545-7580

Ordering Information:
Quantity sales. Special discounts are available on quantity purchases by corporations, associations, and others. For details, contact the publisher at the address above.

Printed in the United States of America.

ISBN-13:   Softcover   979-8-89676-175-4
                  eBook   979-8-89676-176-1

Library of Congress Control Number: 2025911684

TABLE OF CONTENTS

DEDICATION

To my grandmother, Adell McMillan, thank you for being an example of a mother who had unwavering faith, trusted God through the impossible, and exemplified a graceful approach to parenting. Thank you for training me as a child on the importance of personal relationships and encounters with God. Thank you for the late-night check-ins, constant prayers, and stepping in without judgment on my behalf, no matter the circumstance.

To every single mother who has ever cried behind closed doors, whispered prayers of exhaustion, or questioned whether they were enough, this is for you. To the mothers who show up daily, even when their hearts are heavy and their strength is running low, to those who carry the weight of two, who sacrifice, who love fiercely, and who press on when no one is watching. This book is dedicated to you because your efforts are seen, your struggles matter, and your journey is not walked alone.

INTRODUCTION

Becoming a single parent is rarely part of anyone's plan. No one dreams of raising children alone, carrying the weight of two, and navigating life's uncertainties without a partner. Yet, here you are! Whether through divorce, the passing of a spouse, abandonment, or circumstances beyond your control, The road to single parenthood is often filled with uncertainty, exhaustion, and moments of deep struggle. It may feel unfair, overwhelming and at times, unbearably lonely.

The sleepless nights filled with worries about the tasks of the next day, the fatigue from doing it all, the financial pressures, the self-doubt; these struggles are real. You're not alone in these feelings. I, too, share these experiences and feelings due to unexpectedly becoming a single mother in my late 20s. And while society often praises the resilience single mothers are forced to have, the truth is no one should have to carry such burdens alone.

But here's the good news: we don't have to.

Thankfully, God does not expect parents to walk this journey alone. God sees you. He knows your pain, your fears, and your weariness. And even in the moments when you feel forgotten, He is there, ready to walk with you through the valleys of single parenthood. He offers His strength to the weary, His wisdom to the confused, and His peace to the overwhelmed. When the burden feels too heavy, He invites parents to lean on Him. When everything around you feels unstable, God offers unshakable strength. When loneliness creeps in, His presence brings comfort. When you don't know how to move forward, His wisdom lights the way. This journey is not easy, but it can be one of deep transformation. In your weakest moments, you will find God's power sustaining you. In your hardest battles, His grace will equip you, and in the midst of what feels like a loss, He will reveal purpose.

This book offers practical tips, heartfelt prayers, and scriptural encouragement to help you parent intentionally with faith. But the ultimate guide to single parenting lies in God's Word. As you continue through this book you will find if you keep returning to the Bible, you will find wisdom, strength, and inspiration. It is there that you will find the guidance to raise children who love God, love others, and step into the world with purpose and grace.

Chapter 1
Be A Role Model

As a single mother, I constantly battled with self-guilt, questioning whether I was doing enough or making the right choices for my children. There were moments when I felt overwhelmed, wondering if my decisions were truly what was best for their future, or if I was simply trying to juggle too many things at once. I wanted to be a good role model, but it was hard when I was weighed down by the stigma society placed on single mothers, judging, assuming, and sometimes even pitying. That pressure, combined with my internal doubts, made it challenging to stay motivated. Some days, I pushed through with strength, but other times, the exhaustion and self-doubt surfaced, making me feel like I was falling short. It was easy to get caught up in the negative self-talk that said, "You're not enough" or "You'll never measure up." I wanted to show my children resilience, confidence, and self-worth, but teaching them to believe in themselves became even more challenging when I struggled to believe in myself.

When self-doubt and fear of judgement surfaced, I sought God, leaning into His strength when mine felt depleted. I prayed for wisdom, peace, and the grace to show up even when I felt like falling short. I reminded myself that He had called me to this role, and through Him, I could be the mother my children needed, not perfect, but faithful, loving, and constantly growing. These are the exact moments when we should not lean on our strength or understanding but instead intentionally seek God. He knows the depths of our exhaustion and is always there to renew our spirits. So, I did not fear presenting the Lord with all my concerns and asking Him to replace my weariness with comfort and peace.

Children naturally look up to their parents, absorbing behaviors, attitudes, and reactions to everyday situations. Their minds are like sponges, constantly taking in what we do and say. Mothers who demonstrate kindness, patience, and integrity set the tone for their children's behavior, shaping their character and decision-making. If we were honest, after a long night of comforting a teething child followed by a stressful day at work, modeling patience for a child's endless "Why Mama?" questions don't come as easily as we would like. There were days when I felt like I was running on empty, struggling to keep it together, and it was in these moments that my character was tested the most.

Being a role model is essential to being a single mother and a follower of Christ. God calls us to lead by example, showing others, especially our children, how to live in a way that honors Him. We are called not only to teach but to embody the values we want to pass on. 1 Corinthians 11:1 (NIV) says, "Follow my example, as I follow the example of Christ." This means believers should reflect Jesus' character in their daily lives. As our perfect Father, God shows love, patience, and righteousness; single mothers should try to do the same. It's not about perfection but about making consistent efforts to reflect God's love, even on the days when we feel less than perfect. When mothers speak and act with kindness, honesty, and faith, they give their children a strong foundation for life.

Jesus is the most incredible role model, showing love, humility, and obedience to God. In John 13:15 (NIV), Jesus says, "I have set you an example that you should do as I have done for you." He showed servant leadership by washing His disciples' feet, teaching that true leaders serve others with love. Mothers can follow this by being kind, patient, and honest in their daily lives. Instead of just telling their children how to behave, they can show them how to solve problems, treat others, and keep their faith strong through their actions. Children learn more from what they see than what they are told, so when mothers live like Christ, they set an example their children can follow in their faith journey.

Let's look at some examples of how one can be a good role model and how it can benefit both mothers and children.

Teaching Conflict Resolution Through Calm Communication:

Sagine, a mother of an 8-year-old boy named Lucas, noticed Lucas often became frustrated and lashed out when things didn't go his way. One day, while shopping together, Sagine encountered a rude cashier who was visibly impatient. Instead of responding harshly, Sagine said, "I understand you're having a busy day, but I appreciate your help." After observing the interaction, Lucas later asked his mother why she wasn't upset. Sagine explained, "Sometimes people have bad days, and kindness can improve things instead of reacting to her rude behavior which can make things worst. Staying calm and polite shows respect, even when things aren't perfect." A few weeks later, Lucas applied what he learned from his mother when a classmate took his pencil. Instead of yelling, he calmly asked for it back and explained why it was necessary to respect others' belongings. Sagine's consistent example of handling conflict with patience and respect taught Lucas how to approach similar situations in his own life, fostering emotional maturity and empathy.

Emotional Maturity and Empathy - James 1:19-20 (NIV) states "My dear brothers and sisters, take note of this: Everyone should be quick to listen, slow to speak and slow to become angry, because human anger does not produce the righteousness that God desires." Sagine's approach models biblical wisdom and shows Liam how to handle conflict in a way that aligns with God's righteousness.

Demonstrating Perseverance Through Challenges:

Emily, a mom of two, was learning to bake bread from scratch. She involved her 10-year-old daughter, Chloe, in the process. The first few attempts didn't go well; the bread came out too dense or didn't rise properly. Instead of giving up or becoming noticeably angry by slamming things or using harsh language, Emily laughed at the mistakes, tried again, and said, "It's okay to fail as long as we learn something from it." Chloe saw her mom's perseverance and positive attitude, even when things didn't go as planned.

This inspired her when she faced challenges at school, like struggling with a problematic art project. Remembering her mom's words, Chloe approached her teacher for help, practiced more at home, and eventually created a piece she was proud of. By responding with joy and laughter, Emily displays the crucial biblical principle to her daughter Chloe: failure isn't something to fear but an opportunity to grow.

Joy in Trials – The Bible teaches that trials and challenges help us grow. James 1:2-4 (NIV) says, "Consider it pure joy, my brothers and sisters, whenever you face trials of many kinds because you know that the testing of your faith produces perseverance." Emily's joyful response to failure models this biblical principle by showing Chloe that setbacks are growth opportunities.

KEY TAKEAWAYS

★ **Children Learn by Watching**: Actions speak louder than words. When mothers model positive behavior, children internalize these lessons and apply them in their own lives.

★ **Emotional and Social Skills:** Demonstrating patience, kindness, and perseverance helps children build emotional intelligence, empathy, and the ability to handle challenges effectively.

★ **Benefits for Mothers:** For mothers, being a good role model strengthens the parent-child bond and serves as a personal reminder to live authentically and align actions with values. It's rewarding to see the impact of their example reflected in their children's growth and behavior.

★ **Benefits for Children:** For children, having a role model who exemplifies positive behavior builds their confidence, teaches problem-solving skills, and shapes their character. It gives them a practical blueprint for handling life's ups and downs with grace and integrity.

REFLECTIVE QUESTIONS

★   What habits or behaviors do I want my child to emulate?

_____

_____

_____

_____

_____

_____

_____

★   How can I demonstrate patience and kindness more effectively?

_____

_____

_____

_____

_____

_____

_____

_____

★ Am I consistent in my actions and words?

_____

_____

_____

_____

_____

_____

_____

_____

AFFIRMATIONS

My actions teach my child more than my words ever could.

I strive to live the values I want my child to carry.

Every choice I make is an opportunity to inspire my child.

I lead with love, patience, and integrity.

My child learns kindness by watching me give it freely.

I show my child how to handle mistakes with grace.

I model respect so my child will know how to give and receive it.

I demonstrate the courage to be myself so my child feels safe to do the same.

I live my life in a way that I'd be proud to see my child imitate.

I choose my words carefully, knowing little ears are listening.

I model healthy self-care so my child learns the importance of it.

I am shaping the future by showing my child how to live today.

I embody the faith, strength, and compassion I want to see in my child.

I am mindful that my presence teaches as much as my parenting.

Through my example, I am giving my child the tools to thrive.

BIBLE VERSES

★ "Start children off on the way they should go, and even when they are old, they will not turn from it." Proverbs 22:6 (NIV)

★ "For this you have been called, because Christ also suffered for you, leaving you an example, so that you might follow in his steps." 1 Peter 2:21 (ESV)

★ "In everything, set them an example by doing what is good." Titus 2:7 (NIV)

★ "Whatever you have learned or received or heard from me, or seen in me—put it into practice." Philippians 4:9 (NIV)

PRAYER

Heavenly Father,

Thank You for the gift of motherhood and for entrusting me with their precious lives. Help me to be a reflection of Your love and character in every part of my life. Grant me the wisdom to lead by example and the strength to demonstrate values that align with Your will. Teach me to respond with kindness and patience, even when life feels overwhelming. When I face challenges or make mistakes, please help me model humility and resilience so my children learn to grow through life's ups and downs.

Guide me in creating a home filled with compassion, honesty, and faith. Let my words build them up, and my actions inspire them to follow You. Help me to show them how to trust in You in all circumstances and to rely on Your grace and mercy. May they see Your light in my actions and learn to walk confidently in Your truth. Please fill me with the love, patience, and wisdom I need to be the role model they deserve.

In Jesus' name, Amen

CHAPTER 2
Set Clear Boundaries

Single parents often struggle to create and set clear boundaries with their children. Many single mothers have a fear of rejection mindset connected to boundary setting, where they worry if they create structure and limits within their home, their child will feel rejected or become noticeably distant towards them. This fear is not uncommon, as we often want to be seen as loving and nurturing, and setting boundaries can sometimes feel like we are being too harsh or distant. I often failed to be consistent with boundary setting for my oldest child because I frequently felt overwhelmed and irritable. Without a partner to share parenting responsibilities, I often felt overburdened and stretched thin. Others may unconsciously repeat patterns they saw within their homes during their upbringing where no clear boundaries were set. As a result, they may not understand the importance of setting clear boundaries for their children and unknowingly place them at a disadvantage during their adult years. Children need boundaries to feel safe and to grow in wisdom.

When inconsistency with boundary setting arose, I reminded myself that I did not have to rely on my understanding; I could seek God, and He would provide me with the guidance I needed. I did this by praying to Him, laying my worries at His feet, and asking for clarity. I opened my Bible and meditated on His promises, like James 1:5 (NIV), which reminded me that if I lacked wisdom, I only needed to ask, and He would give it generously. This verse was such a source of comfort for me. It is a reminder that I did not need to have all the answers, just the willingness to seek God's wisdom. I tried to quiet my anxious thoughts and listen for His direction, whether through scripture, a sermon, or the gentle nudge of the Holy Spirit. Above all, I chose to trust Him and believe that even when I felt lost, He was already making a way. I reminded myself that He saw my struggles, knew my heart, and would provide the wisdom and strength needed.

Setting clear and consistent boundaries is essential for a child's development. Children who understand what's expected of them feel secure and learn accountability. Explaining the reasons behind the rules helps them internalize these boundaries, fostering self-discipline and a sense of responsibility. I've found that when I can calmly explain why certain rules are in place, my children are more likely to understand and comply. When boundaries are set without explanation, it can feel arbitrary and confusing to a child.

Setting clear boundaries is vital to creating order, wisdom, and healthy relationships, just as God intended. Throughout the Bible, God sets boundaries to protect and guide His people. Proverbs 4:23 (NIV) says, "Above all else, guard your heart, for everything you do flows from it." This reminds us that setting limits helps protect our spiritual, emotional, and physical well-being. God's commandments, like the Ten Commandments (Exodus 20), serve as guidelines to help people live correctly and avoid harmful choices.

Jesus also showed the importance of boundaries in His life and ministry. He was loving and compassionate but also knew when to set limits. In Mark 1:35-38, He took time to pray alone, even when people were looking for Him, showing that He prioritized rest and spiritual renewal. He also stood firm when needed, like in Matthew 21:12-13, when He cleared the temple of wrongdoing. We can follow Jesus' example by setting healthy boundaries with our children. This means teaching them to respect authority, take responsibility for their actions, and value rest and spiritual growth. When we set firm but loving boundaries, we help our children develop self-discipline and a clear understanding of right and wrong, preparing them to live with faith and wisdom.

As single mothers, we can follow this example by setting clear and loving rules for our children. Boundaries teach discipline, respect, and self-control. Just as God's laws are meant to help us, the boundaries we set for our children provide them with security and direction, shaping them into responsible and God-honoring individuals.

Let's look at some examples of how setting clear boundaries, God's way, provides tremendous benefit to both children and mothers.

Creating a Bedtime Routine for Young Children:

Sophia, a mother of a 4-year-old named Bri'elle, struggled with bedtime battles. Bri'elle often resisted going to bed, asking for "just one more story," or staying up late playing games on her iPad. Sophia realized that the lack of a consistent routine created stress for both of them and needed to be changed.

Sophia decided to set a clear bedtime boundary and routine. She explained to Bri'elle, "You need sleep to grow healthy and strong, and staying up too late can make it hard for your body to rest. From now on, bedtime will be at 7:30 p.m. That means we'll bathe, brush our teeth, read one story, and then it's lights out."

At first, Bri'elle resisted the change, crying uncontrollably for "one more story" and time to play on her iPad. Still, Sophia stayed consistent, calmly reminding Bri'elle of the new routine each night with gentleness. Within a week, Bri'elle began to accept the structure, and bedtime became less of a struggle and more enjoyable for Sarah and Bri'elle. As a result, Bri'elle started waking up feeling more refreshed and was more focused during school. Sophia also benefited from having a predictable evening routine. Since Bri'elle was in bed, it gave her some quiet time to recharge. This experience showed her how setting boundaries created a sense of security for Bri'elle and reduced stress for the entire family.

Endurance and Growth through Change – Change can be challenging, but Romans 12:2 (NIV) teaches, "Do not be conformed to this world but be transformed by the renewal of your mind." The passage emphasizes that although change may be difficult, consistency and the right approach can lead to positive transformation, as Sophia demonstrates.

Establishing Screen Time Limits for Older Children:

Carmelo, a 12-year-old, spent hours playing video games after school on his iPad, often neglecting his homework and chores. Over time, his mom, Karenah, noticed the negative impact on his school performance and family interactions. Karenah sat down with Carmelo and explained, "I understand how much you enjoy your games, but spending too much time on your tablet takes away from other important things, like your homework, helping around the house, and spending time together as a family. Let's set some rules to ensure you have a healthy balance."

They agreed on a rule: one hour of screen time after school, but only after homework and chores were completed on weekdays. Karenah also involved Carmelo in creating a schedule to help him manage his time. At first, Carmelo pushed back, but Karenah stood firm and consistent, gently reminding Carmelo of the rules they had created and implemented together as many times as needed. Over time, Carmelo adapted to the new regulations and completed his responsibilities before enjoying his screen time. Over time, Karenah noticed a positive change: Carmelo's grades improved, and he became more engaged during family activities.

This experience reinforced for Karenah that clear boundaries, paired with explanations and collaboration, not only taught Carmelo accountability but also strengthened their relationship by showing mutual respect.

<u>Collaboration and Wisdom</u> – Proverbs 27:17 (NIV) states, "As iron sharpens iron, so one person sharpens another." Karenah's approach strengthens her relationship with Carmelo, showing wisdom and growth through guidance and cooperation.

KEY TAKEAWAYS

★ **Promotes Security and Predictability:** Clear boundaries give children a sense of stability, helping them understand what is expected and reducing anxiety.

★ **Teaches Responsibility and Accountability:** Explaining the reasons behind rules encourages children to see boundaries as a way to learn self-discipline rather than restrictions.

★ **Benefits for Mothers:** Setting boundaries reduces conflicts and creates a more harmonious household. It allows them to guide their children effectively while fostering trust and respect. By staying consistent and explaining the "why" behind the rules, mothers help their children grow into responsible and well-adjusted individuals.

★ **Benefits for Children:** Clear and consistent boundaries offer a framework for making good choices, developing self-discipline, and feeling secure. They learn to respect rules and understand their reasoning, which helps them develop critical thinking and accountability.

REFLECTIVE QUESTIONS

★ Are my expectations for my child reasonable and age-appropriate?

_____

_____

_____

_____

_____

_____

_____

★ How do I enforce boundaries without being overly harsh?

_____

_____

_____

_____

_____

_____

_____

★ Do I explain rules in a way that is understanding?

_____

_____

_____

_____

_____

_____

_____

_____

_____

AFFIRMATIONS

My boundaries teach my child how to respect themselves and others.

Saying "no" when needed is an act of love and protection.

I can be compassionate and firm at the same time.

I honor my needs so I can better care for my child's needs.

Clear boundaries create a safe and trusting home.

It's okay for my child to feel disappointed when I hold my limits.

I am my child's guide, not their doormat.

Respect is a two-way street in our family.

I model self-respect through the boundaries I set.

Love is stronger when it's supported by healthy limits.

I am not responsible for making my child happy at the cost of my well-being.

Firm boundaries today create responsible adults tomorrow.

I can hold my boundary without guilt.

Boundaries are an expression of love, not rejection.

My "no" is just as valuable as my "yes."

BIBLE VERSES

★ "Because the Lord disciplines those he loves, as a father the son he delights in." Proverbs 3:12 (NIV)

★ "For the moment, all discipline seems painful rather than pleasant, but later, it yields the peaceful fruit of righteousness to those who have been trained by it." Hebrews 12:11 (ESV)

★ "Fathers, do not exasperate your children; instead, bring them up in the training and instruction of the Lord." Ephesians 6:4 (NIV)

★ "How can a young person stay on the path of purity? By living according to your word." Psalms 119:9 (NIV)

PRAYER

Heavenly Father,

Guide me as I set boundaries for my children. Help me to be firm but loving, consistent but compassionate. Let these boundaries reflect Your truth and provide a foundation for my children growth. Give me patience when they test limits and wisdom to handle each situation with grace. Help me explain the reasons behind my decisions so they understand and learn. Let our home be a place where structure and love coexist, and where they feel secure to thrive within the boundaries I set.

Thank You for the gift of motherhood and for entrusting me with their precious lives. May Your Spirit fill me with the love, patience, and wisdom I need to be the consistent parent they deserve.

In Jesus' name, Amen.

CHAPTER 3
Communicate Effectively

As a single mother, there were times when I struggled to communicate effectively with my child. I sometimes felt lost, unsure if I was saying the right things or handling situations the best way. I often second-guessed myself, questioning whether I was being clear enough or if my words were making an impact. There was no one to step in, offer guidance, reassurance or wisdom, and the weight of making every decision alone often felt overwhelming. I felt the burden of shaping my children's world, teaching them right from wrong, and guiding them through every stage of development all without another person to share that responsibility.

When uncertainty arose, I reminded myself He was my ultimate source of strength and peace. When I felt unsure of what to say, I prayed for patience, clarity, and the ability to speak to my child in a way that nurtured, uplifted, and guide them. I reminded myself that I didn't need to have all the answers because God did. Effective communication is essential for fostering a strong and healthy relationship between a mother and her children. I learned that when I surrendered my anxieties and allowed Him to lead, my communication became more thoughtful, loving, and aligned with His will. By actively listening, slowly God helped me shift my approach to communicating in a way my child understood rather than how I naturally express myself. I learned by actively listening, showing empathy, and encouraging open dialogue between my child and I, it created an environment where she felt heard, valued, and understood. As a result, trust was built and I helped develop confidence and emotional resilience.

Effective communication is essential to building strong relationships, and we can see this clearly in how God and Jesus communicate with people in the Bible. God speaks to His people through His Word, guiding them with love, wisdom, and truth. In James 1:19, the Bible says, "Everyone should be quick to listen, slow to speak, and slow to become angry." This teaches us that good communication involves listening carefully and responding with patience. Single Mothers can follow this example by listening to their children, speaking with kindness, and using words to encourage rather than tear down. Just as God communicates with love and clarity, single mothers can build trust with their children by speaking truthfully and with understanding.

Jesus was also a master communicator, using parables and simple language to teach profound truths. He spoke in a way people could understand, meeting them where they were. Matthew 13:34 (ESV) says, "Jesus spoke all these things to the crowd in parables." He asked questions, listened to people's concerns, and responded with wisdom and compassion. Mothers can follow His example by ensuring their words are clear, loving, and uplifting. When mothers communicate effectively, listen with patience, correct with love, and speak truth with kindness, they create a home where children feel heard, valued, and guided in the right direction.

Let's look at some examples of how communicating effectively provides tremendous benefits to both children and mothers.

Navigating a Difficult Friendship Situation:

Kyieta, the mother of a 10-year-old girl named Gwen, noticed Gwen was unusually quiet after school one day. When Kyieta gently asked if everything was okay, Gwen hesitated but eventually said, "I don't think my best friend likes me anymore. She's been spending more time with someone else, and I feel left out."

Instead of immediately offering solutions or dismissing Gwen's feelings, Kyieta practiced active listening. She said, "That sounds hard. It must hurt to feel like things are changing between you two." This empathetic response made Gwen feel understood and encouraged her to share more. As Gwen talked, Kyieta asked open-ended questions like, "What do you think might be going on?" and "How do you want to handle this?" Together, they brainstormed ways Gwen could talk to her friend about her feelings. Kyieta reminded Gwen that friendships sometimes shift but also emphasized the importance of expressing emotions in a kind and honest way.

A few days later, Gwen shared with her mom that she had spoken to her friend and felt better. Kyieta realized that by simply listening and offering guidance without judgment, she had helped Gwen navigate the situation independently while reinforcing their bond. This experience taught Gwen that she could turn to her mom for support without fear of being dismissed or misunderstood.

Trusting in a Safe Refuge – Psalm 46:1 (NIV) says, "God is our refuge and strength, an ever-present help in trouble." Just as God is a refuge for His people, Gwen learns that her mother is a safe place to turn to, mirroring believers' trust and comfort in their relationship with God.

Addressing School Stress Through Open Dialogue:

Ethan, a 14-year-old, started coming home from school looking stressed and irritable. His mom, Liz, noticed the change in his demeanor but resisted the urge to pry. Instead, she chose a calm moment to say, "I've noticed you've seemed a bit stressed lately. Is there something on your mind?" Ethan initially brushed her off with a vague "I'm fine," but Liz persisted gently. She said, "I'm here to listen if you want to talk. I remember how tough school could be at your age." By sharing her experiences, Liz created a safe space for Ethan to open up.

Later that evening, Ethan approached her and admitted he was struggling with an upcoming math test and felt overwhelmed by expectations to perform well. Liz listened without interrupting and validated his feelings, saying, "It's normal to feel anxious when you're under pressure. I'm proud of you for sharing this with me." Together, they discussed ways Ethan could manage his stress, like breaking his study sessions into smaller chunks, taking breaks, and asking his teacher for extra help. Liz also assured Ethan that her love and pride in him weren't tied to his grades.

By encouraging open dialogue, Liz helped Ethan manage his immediate stress and taught him that seeking help and expressing vulnerability is okay. Over time, Ethan became more comfortable sharing his thoughts and feelings with his mom, strengthening their relationship.

The Power of Open Communication: Speaking honestly and sharing emotions fosters more profound relationships. Proverbs 15:1 (ESV) "A soft answer turns away wrath, but a harsh word stirs up anger." Liz's approach of encouraging open dialogue allows Ethan to express his feelings without fear, reinforcing trust and understanding.

KEY TAKEAWAYS

★ **Building Emotional Security**: Open and empathetic communication helps children feel safe and valued, fostering trust and emotional security.

★ **Teaching Problem-Solving Skills:** When mothers listen actively and guide without imposing, they empower children to think critically and find their solutions.

★ **Benefits for Mothers:** For mothers, clear communication models emotional intelligence, advocacy of your needs, reduces stress, sets healthy boundaries and creates deeper, more meaningful relationships.

★ **Benefits for Children:** For children, effective communication provides a foundation of trust, allowing them to express themselves freely and confidently. It helps them feel seen and understood, boosting their self-esteem and emotional well-being.

REFLECTIVE QUESTIONS

★   Do I actively listen to my child without interrupting?

_____

_____

_____

_____

_____

_____

_____

_____

★   How can I improve my tone and approach during difficult conversations?

_____

_____

_____

_____

_____

_____

_____

_____

_____

★ Am I fostering an atmosphere of trust and openness?

_____

_____

_____

_____

_____

_____

_____

_____

AFFIRMATIONS

I listen to my child with my heart as well as my ears.

I create a safe space for my child to share their thoughts and feelings.

My words build trust and connection with my child.

I speak with patience, even in moments of frustration.

I choose clarity over criticism when talking to my child.

I validate my child's feelings, even if I don't agree with their choices.

I listen without interrupting so my child feels valued.

My tone shows love, even when I am correcting behavior.

I teach my child that every voice in our home matters.

I am open to learning from my child as much as they learn from me.

I take time to understand before I respond.

I communicate in ways that strengthen our relationship, not weaken it.

I use my words to guide, not to shame.

I am mindful that my child is learning how to communicate by watching me.

Every conversation with my child is a chance to build deeper trust.

BIBLE VERSES

★ "To answer before listening—that is folly and shame." Proverbs 18:13 (NIV)

★ "Know this, my beloved brothers: let every person be quick to hear, slow to speak, slow to anger." James 1:19 (ESV)

★ "Let your conversation be always full of grace, seasoned with salt, so that you may know how to answer everyone." Colossians 4:6 (NIV)

★ "Do not let any unwholesome talk come out of your mouths, but only what helps build others up according to their needs." Ephesians 4:29 (NIV)

PRAYER

Heavenly Father,

I come to You seeking guidance as I strive to be a better communicator with my children. Teach me to listen with my whole heart, to hear not just their words but the emotions and needs behind them. Help me to respond with empathy and understanding, reflecting Your love in every interaction. Give me the patience to pause before I speak and the wisdom to choose words that build up rather than tear down.

Show me how to create an environment where my children feel safe to share their thoughts and feelings. Help me to ask the right questions and to truly hear their answers. When they face challenges, guide me to offer support and solutions rooted in Your truth. When I'm frustrated or tired, remind me to lean on Your strength so I can communicate with grace and love.

Teach me to model honesty and vulnerability so my children learn the value of open and truthful conversations. May my words encourage, uplift, and guide them closer to You. Let our home be a place where communication flows freely, fostering trust and deepening our connection as a family. Fill me with Your Spirit, Lord, so I may reflect Your love and wisdom in all I say and do.

In Jesus' name, Amen.

CHAPTER 4
Show Unconditional Love

As a single mother, showing unconditional love was one of the hardest things I did, not because I didn't love my children, but because everything fell on me. There were days when the exhaustion was unbearable, when the stress of bills became too much to handle, seasons where I was battling emotions I didn't even have time to process, and patience wore thin. Sometimes resentment emerged toward the current state of my life, toward the situation, the absent support, and the dreams I had to put on hold in this season. It was hard to pour from an empty cup, and there were moments when I struggled to separate my frustration from my parenting. I knew that my children didn't deserve my anger or weariness, but it was difficult to manage my emotions when I felt so alone on this journey.

When I struggled to manage my emotions, I learned to surrender all my emotions to the Lord. I also learned to extend grace to myself because, as a single mother, I was carrying out a role intended by God to be shared with a partner. I came to realize that these moments of frustration were not a reflection of my love for my children, but rather the result of carrying such a heavy load without rest. I learned that it was okay to admit that I wasn't always okay and that it was important to give myself grace. As a result, there were times when I made mistakes and was short-tempered with my children, although it was unwarranted, and to be completely transparent, I had given up. I am so glad God met me during those low moments and restored my strength, peace, and wisdom to continue to care for my children lovingly. Also, I was grateful that while wholeheartedly coming to Him in prayer; He reminded me that He has equipped me for a time such as this, and the battle was already won!

Unconditional love is the cornerstone of effective parenting. It gives children a sense of security, self-worth, and confidence, knowing their value doesn't depend on their achievements or behavior. I've come to see that even on my hardest days, my children still need to feel my love, regardless of what's going on in my life or how I'm feeling. No matter what, mothers have to create a nurturing environment where children can thrive emotionally and socially by consistently demonstrating unwavering and not performance-based love. Children are intuitive. They can feel the difference when love is conditional, based on their behavior or achievements. When love is unconditional, it allows them the freedom to make mistakes, learn, and grow without fear of rejection or disapproval.

Jesus and God exemplify unconditional love through grace, forgiveness, and sacrifice. Jesus demonstrated this love by healing the sick, embracing the outcasts, and ultimately sacrificing His life on the cross for humanity's sins. God's love is unwavering, offering redemption and second chances regardless of mistakes. This divine love is not based on merit but given freely, reminding us that true love is patient, kind, and never failing.

Single mothers can model this unconditional love by showing their children patience, forgiveness, and unwavering support. Just as God accepts us despite our flaws, parents can extend grace when their children make mistakes, guiding them with wisdom instead of harsh judgment. By providing a safe, loving environment where children feel valued and accepted, parents reflect the kind of love God and Jesus demonstrate, one that nurtures, encourages, and never gives up.

Let's look at some examples of how showing unconditional love provides tremendous benefits to both children and mothers.

Supporting a Child Through Academic Struggles:

Keylah, a mother of an 11-year-old named Amir, noticed her son struggling with math. Despite his efforts, Amir received a poor grade on a test and came home feeling defeated. He said, "I'm just not good at math. I'll never be as smart as my classmates."

Keylah saw this as an opportunity to show unconditional love and support. She sat with Amir and said, "Your grades don't change how much I love you. I'm proud of you for trying your best, and we'll work together to figure this out." She reminded him of his strengths in other areas, like his creativity in art and his enthusiasm for science projects.

Keylah then helped Amir develop a plan to improve, including extra practice and seeking help from his teacher. Over time, Amir began to make progress. What stuck with him, however, was not just his improvement in math but the reassurance that his mom's love didn't depend on his grades. He grew more resilient, knowing he could face challenges without fear of losing her support. For Keylah, this experience reinforced the importance of showing Amir that his worth wasn't tied to his performance, helping him develop a stronger self-esteem.

<u>Self-Worth Beyond Performance</u> – Keylah teaches Amir that his worth is not tied to his achievements, which aligns with God's perspective on our value as shown in Psalms 139:13-14 (NIV) which states "For you created my inmost being; you knit me together in my mother's womb. I praise you because I am fearfully and wonderfully made; your works are wonderful; I know that full well."

Nurturing Emotional Security After a Mistake:

Adell, a mother of a 7-year-old girl named Olivia, faced a challenging parenting moment when Olivia accidentally broke her grandmother's favorite vase while playing indoors. Olivia was visibly upset and kept apologizing, saying, "I know you're mad at me. I didn't mean to do it!"

Instead of focusing on the broken vase, Adell hugged Olivia, saying, "I know it was an accident. What matters to me is that you're okay, and I love you no matter what." Adell used the situation to teach Olivia about responsibility, calmly explaining why playing with a ball inside wasn't a good idea.

Later, Adell and Olivia worked together to clean up the mess, and Adell suggested they write an apology note to Grandma. This moment reassured Olivia that her mom's love wasn't conditional on her behavior, and it gave her the confidence to admit her mistakes and take responsibility without fear. For Adell, it was a reminder of the power of compassion and patience in building emotional security in her daughter.

Taking Responsibility and Confession: Olivia's ability to admit her mistake connects to 1 John 1:9 (NIV) "If we confess our sins, he is faithful and just and will forgive us our sins and purify us from all unrighteousness." Just as Olivia took responsibility for her actions and was reassured by unconditional love, the Bible teaches that when we confess our wrongdoings, God will forgive us.

KEY TAKEAWAYS

★ **Building Emotional Resilience:** Unconditional love gives children the courage to face challenges and setbacks, knowing they are valued for who they are, not for what they achieve or behave.

★ **Fostering a Safe Environment:** When children feel loved without conditions, they are more likely to open up about their fears, mistakes, and struggles, strengthening the parent-child bond.

★ **Benefits for Children:** For children, Unconditional love creates trust and security, helping children develop confidence, emotional intelligence, and a healthy sense of self-worth.

★ **Benefits for Mothers:** It fosters more profound connections with their children, allowing them to guide and nurture from a place of compassion and understanding. By showing your child that your love is unwavering, even in difficult moments, you equip them with the emotional tools they need to grow into resilient and self-assured individuals.

REFLECTIVE QUESTIONS

★ How do I express love during moments of discipline?

_____

_____

_____

_____

_____

_____

_____

_____

★ Does my child know that my love is not conditional?

_____

_____

_____

_____

_____

_____

_____

_____

★ How can I show love in ways that resonate with my child's unique personality?

_____

_____

_____

_____

_____

_____

_____

_____

_____

AFFIRMATIONS

My love for my child is steady, constant, and unwavering.

I love my child for who they are, not just for what they do.

Nothing my child does can make me stop loving them.

I cherish my child through every season of life.

My love embraces my child's strengths and imperfections.

I see my child's value and worth, always.

Even in tough moments, my love remains unshaken.

I celebrate my child's unique spirit every day.

I love my child not because they are perfect, but because they are mine.

My child never has to earn my love; it is already theirs.

I am grateful every day for the gift of my child.

My love is the safe place my child can always return to.

I love my child through mistakes, growth, and change.

I hold space for my child's feelings without judgment.

My child is deeply loved, no matter what happens in life.

BIBLE VERSES

★ "But God demonstrates his love for us in this: While we were still sinners, Christ died for us." Romans 5:8 (NIV)

★ "[Love] bears all things, believes all things, hopes all things, endures all things." 1 Corinthians 13:7 (ESV)

★ "We love because he first loved us." 1 John 4:19 (NIV)

★ "As a father has compassion on his children, so the Lord has compassion on those who fear him." Psalms 103:13 (NIV)

PRAYER

Heavenly Father,

I come to You with a heart longing to love my children as You love me unconditionally and without measure. Teach me to see beyond their actions and into their hearts, to love them for who they are, not for what they do. Please help me to show grace in moments of frustration and to respond with patience and understanding, even when I feel overwhelmed. My children are, cherished and love by me. My home is filled with love. I am my children's safe place. I can love my children like Jesus loves me.

Help me to remember daily that my love should reflect Your steadfastness and unwavering love. When my children face challenges or make mistakes, please give me the wisdom to guide them gently and the strength to be their constant support. Let my words and actions assure them they are valued, cherished, and loved beyond measure, no matter the circumstances.

Help me create a home where love is the foundation, and they feel safe to grow, learn, and thrive. May my love point them to You, Lord, so they may come to know and trust in Your perfect love. Help me to love my child in the same way, showing grace, patience, and forgiveness. Let my love reflect Your heart.

In Jesus' name, Amen.

Chapter 5

Encourage Independence

As a single parent, I often found myself doing things for my children because it was easier and faster at the time. Whether making sure school lunch was packed for the next day or taking care of chores around the house. But I realized that by doing this, I was unintentionally teaching my child to rely on me instead of encouraging independence. It felt like the best choice in the short term, but over time, it became a crutch for both of us. I was overworking myself, and my children weren't developing the skills to manage tasks or solve problems independently. It was easy to fall into this trap of wanting to shield my child from struggles, but I knew that part of my job as a parent was to prepare them for the future. It was a balancing act of trying to provide for them while teaching them how to stand on their own two feet.

When impatience crept in towards my children, I turned to God asking Him for patience and wisdom at the time. I asked God to help me see my children's struggles through His eyes and with love and understanding rather than irritation. When I felt like I was failing, I reminded myself that God has always been patient with me, so I must extend that patience to my children. I reminded myself that the struggles my children faced were not burdens but opportunities for growth. Each challenge they encountered was a chance for them to learn, build resilience, and gain confidence in their ability to handle life's hurdles.

When frustration rose, I paused, took a deep breath, and whispered a simple prayer: "Lord, help me teach with grace, not impatience." I reflected on scriptures like Proverbs 22:6 (NIV), which reminded me to train my child in the way they should go, knowing that these small lessons would shape their future.

When I was unsure how to balance support with independence, I trusted He would give me the wisdom to guide my children in a way that built confidence and resilience without losing my peace. I also learned to remind myself that my role was to guide, not control.

Encouraging independence in your children is one of the most impactful ways to prepare them for the future. By teaching them how to make decisions, solve problems, and take responsibility for their actions, you build their confidence, resilience, and ability to handle challenges gracefully and competently. These life skills are essential for their emotional and mental well-being, and they are foundational for success in adulthood. This guidance also allows them to grow into self-reliant individuals while strengthening the bond between you as they learn to trust your support and wisdom.

Jesus taught independence through faith and personal responsibility. He encouraged people to seek God directly, make moral choices, and take ownership of their actions. His parables, such as The Prodigal Son, highlight the balance between guidance and allowing individuals to learn from experience. By teaching His disciples to go out on their own and spread His message, Jesus modeled independence through trust and empowerment.

God, as a loving Father, provides guidance but also allows free will, teaching that genuine growth comes from personal choices. Parents can model this by setting expectations, offering wisdom, and stepping back to let their children navigate challenges. Just as God gives His children the freedom to learn and grow, parents can foster independence by encouraging problem-solving, resilience, and faith-driven decision-making.

Let's look at examples of how encouraging independence benefits both children and mothers.

Teaching Problem-Solving Through Real-Life Challenges:

Charlotte, a mother of a 9-year-old boy named Rodney, noticed that Rodney often struggled to manage his school projects. He would get overwhelmed and rely on Charlotte to organize everything for him. One day, Charlotte decided it was time to help Rodney take more responsibility for his work.

When Rodney received a new science project, Charlotte sat down with him and guided him through breaking it into smaller, manageable steps. She asked him, "What's the first thing we need to do?" and "How can we ensure everything is done on time?" Rodney devised a plan to research his topic, gather materials, and allocate specific days to work on each part of the project. Charlotte supervised from the sidelines, offering encouragement but allowing Rodney to make his own decisions.

Rodney proudly presented his project at school and received positive feedback; his confidence soared. He realized he was capable of managing tasks on his own. Charlotte, in turn, felt proud of her son's progress and recognized how fostering his independence empowered him to tackle challenges with a sense of ownership.

Hard Work and Confidence in One's Abilities – Rodney's experience reflects the biblical teaching that diligence leads to success. Proverbs 22:29 (NKJV): "Do you see a man who excels in his work? He will stand before kings; He will not stand before unknown men." Rodney's hard work on his project and the positive feedback he received mirror the principle that excellence and dedication bring recognition and growth.

Encouraging Decision-Making in Everyday Situations:

Felicia, a mom to 12-year-old Harper, wanted to teach her daughter how to make thoughtful decisions. When Harper wanted to join two after-school clubs that met on the same day, Felicia used the situation as a learning opportunity.

Instead of deciding for her, Felicia asked Harper to weigh the pros and cons of each club. She said, "Think about which club aligns more with your goals and interests. How will you feel if you choose one over the other?" Felicia listened as Harper discussed her love for art and interest in joining the drama club to meet new friends. After careful consideration, Harper chose the drama club, feeling confident in her decision.

Later, when Harper encountered similar dilemmas, she began applying the decision-making skills she had learned. Felicia noticed that Harper became more thoughtful and proactive in handling choices, big or small. Watching her daughter grow more independent reinforced Felicia's belief in stepping back and letting her child take the lead.

Gaining Wisdom Through Experience – James 1:5 (ESV) states, "If any of you lacks wisdom, let him ask God, who gives generously to all without reproach, and it will be given him." Harper's growth in thoughtful decision-making reflects the biblical encouragement to seek and apply wisdom, which often comes through experience and reflection.

KEY TAKEAWAYS

★   **Encouraging Decision-Making:** Giving children opportunities to make choices helps them learn how to evaluate options, trust their instincts, and take ownership of their decisions.

★   **Teaching Problem-Solving:** Guiding children through challenges instead of solving problems for them equips them with the skills to handle setbacks and find solutions independently.

★   **Benefits for Mothers:** For mothers, encouraging independence helps reduce the stress of constantly making decisions or solving problems for their children. Witnessing their child's growth and capability also brings joy and pride. Most importantly, fostering independence strengthens the parent-child relationship by showing children that their parents trust and believe in their abilities.

★   **Benefits for Children:** For children, learning to make decisions and solve problems fosters self-confidence, critical thinking, and a sense of responsibility. They begin to trust their abilities and feel empowered to take on new challenges.

★   Teaching independence is a gradual process, but the rewards are profound. Children who learn to think for themselves and take responsibility grow into capable, confident, and self-reliant individuals who are prepared to face the world with resilience and determination.

REFLECTIVE QUESTIONS

★ Do I allow my child to make age-appropriate decisions?

_____

_____

_____

_____

_____

_____

_____

_____

★ How can I support my child without being overbearing?

_____

_____

_____

_____

_____

_____

_____

_____

★   Am I teaching responsibility through my expectations and actions?

_____

_____

_____

_____

_____

_____

_____

_____

_____

AFFIRMATIONS

I trust my child to explore and learn in their own way.

I give my child space to grow while offering steady support.

I celebrate my child's efforts, not just their outcomes.

I allow my child to make age-appropriate choices for themselves.

I guide without controlling, knowing independence builds confidence.

I encourage my child to solve problems and learn from their experiences.

I am patient as my child learns new skills at their own pace.

I respect my child's voice and their right to express themselves.

I allow my child to try, even if they might stumble.

I model confidence so my child feels secure in their own abilities.

I remind my child that mistakes are stepping stones to growth.

I give my child the tools to succeed and trust them to use them.

I believe in my child's potential to become capable and self-reliant.

I balance guidance with freedom so my child can flourish.

I am proud to watch my child grow into their own person.

BIBLE VERSES

★ "For each one should carry their load." Galatians 6:5 (NIV)

★ "Commit to the Lord whatever you do, and he will establish your plans." Proverbs 16:3 (NIV)

★ "For I know the plans I have for you," declares the Lord, "plans to prosper you and not to harm you, plans to give you hope and a future." Jeremiah 29:11 (NIV)

★ "I can do all this through him who gives me strength." Philippians 4:13 (NIV)

PRAYER

Heavenly Father,

I come to You with a heart that longs to guide my children toward independence while still surrounding them with love and support. Teach me to encourage their growth in a way that reflects Your wisdom and care. Please help me balance stepping in when needed and stepping back to allow them to learn from their choices.

Give me patience when they struggle and wisdom when they seek my guidance. Show me how to nurture their decision-making skills and problem-solving abilities, trusting that these lessons will prepare them for the path You have set before them. Please remind me to celebrate their successes and to offer grace and understanding when they stumble.

Thank You for the incredible blessing of motherhood and for entrusting me with the precious responsibility of raising my children. Thank you for equipping me with the tools I need to teach them independence while remaining a source of unwavering support.

In Jesus' name, Amen.

CHAPTER 6
Practice Positive Discipline

I often struggled with practicing positive discipline when my oldest was young because my emotions took over. The challenges of being a single mother combined with feelings of anger and resentment stemming from stress and the worry of doing it all alone, sometimes made it difficult to stay patient and guide my children in a calm supportive way. There were moments when I reacted out of frustration, rather than teaching with understanding, and I recognized that some of this behavior stemmed from my own upbringing. I sometimes repeated patterns simply because they were all I knew or what I had seen other parents do, even if it didn't always feel right. Instead of responding with intention, I reacted out of habit and fell into the same cycles that once shaped me. Then, I remembered how I felt as a child in those moments. I remembered wishing for more understanding, patience and room to express myself and explain. Those memories humbled me and reminded me that I had the power to break cycles, to parent differently, to learn and grow. I may not have had all the answers, but I could seek wisdom from God and resources that taught me healthier ways to guide my children. I reminded myself that awareness was the first step to change, and even when I fell short, I could do better with each new day.

When worry surfaced, I turned to God and laid my emotions at his feet, instead of letting anger or animosity take over. I learned that it was okay to feel frustrated or upset, but I must not let these emotions dictate my actions. When I felt resentment surface, I surrendered it to God, asking Him to replace it with patience and understanding. I reflected on how He disciplined me with kindness, consistency, and love and strove to model that in my parenting. If I lost my temper, I didn't let guilt consume me; instead, I asked for God's forgiveness and the strength to try again.

Positive discipline is a powerful approach that focuses on teaching children rather than punishing them. It helps them understand the consequences of their actions and learn from their mistakes while maintaining a loving and respectful relationship with their mothers. Positive discipline emphasized the importance of guiding children through their behavior, helping them to see how their actions affected themselves and others. This method encourages better choices, fosters emotional intelligence, builds trust and mutual respect between a mother and her child.

Jesus and God exemplify positive discipline through their teachings of love, patience, and guidance rather than punishment. Jesus, through his parables and actions, corrected and taught with compassion, always offering a path to redemption and growth. God, as a loving Father, disciplines His children not out of anger but to help them grow in wisdom and righteousness (Hebrews 12:6 NIV). Their approach to discipline is rooted in encouragement, mercy, and the desire for transformation rather than mere punishment. Through His discipline, God teaches us valuable lessons about His love, grace, and the path to becoming who He created us to be.

Single mothers can model this behavior by setting clear boundaries with love, correcting their children with patience, and using discipline as a tool for teaching rather than punishment. Just as Jesus gently guided his disciples, mothers can offer correction with kindness, reinforcing positive behavior and teaching through example. I've learned that when I focus on teaching and guiding rather than punishing, I create a safer, more nurturing environment for my children. It's important to set clear expectations and communicate those to my children, but also to remember that mistakes are a part of growing up. By practicing forgiveness, offering second chances, and focusing on growth rather than harsh consequences, this mirrors God's loving discipline, fostering respect, trust, and moral strength in their children.

Let's examine examples of how positive discipline benefits children and mothers.

Teaching Responsibility Through Gentle Correction:

Cassi, the mother of a 4-year-old boy named LeRoyal often struggled with LeRoyal leaving his toys scattered around the house. Instead of yelling or taking the toys away as punishment, Cassi decided to use this as a teaching moment.

One day, when LeRoyal left his toys out again, Cassi calmly sat him down and explained the impact of his actions. She said, "When you leave your toys everywhere, someone could trip and get hurt, or the toys might get lost or broken. Let's find a way to make sure this doesn't happen again."

Together, they brainstormed a solution. LeRoyal suggested creating a unique "toy zone" in the living room where he could keep his toys organized. They worked on setting up the area together, and Cassi praised Ethan for his idea and effort. The next time Ethan forgot to clean up, Cassi gently reminded him, "Remember, we agreed to keep the toys in the toy zone. Let's clean them up together." Over time, LeRoyal took responsibility for tidying up his toys without being asked.

This approach taught LeRoyal about accountability and problem-solving in a way that empowered him rather than making him feel ashamed or resentful. For Cassi, it was rewarding to see her son develop a sense of responsibility while strengthening their bond through collaboration.

Accountability and Growth – The approach that LeRoyal experienced aligns with Galatians 6:5 (NIV) "For each one should carry their own load." This verse emphasizes personal responsibility, teaching that individuals must take ownership of their actions, just as LeRoyal learned to be accountable without feeling ashamed.

Encouraging Better Choices with Constructive Feedback:

Shantel, the mother of a 10-year-old girl named Jackie, faced a challenge when Jackie started interrupting conversations at family gatherings. Instead of scolding Lily in front of others, Shantel decided to address the issue constructively.

After the gathering, Shantel talked privately with Jackie. She said, "I noticed you were excited to share your thoughts today, and that's great. But when you interrupt, it can make others feel like what they're saying isn't important. How about we practice waiting for a pause in the conversation before you speak?"

Shantel role-played a conversation with Jackie, showing her how to wait for a natural break before joining in. She also praised Jackie for her enthusiasm and encouraged her to continue contributing to discussions in a way that allowed everyone to feel heard.

At the next family gathering, Shantel noticed Jackie pausing before speaking. When Jackie waited her turn and shared her thoughts, Shantel gave her positive reinforcement by saying, "I loved how you waited to speak today. It made the conversation so much better for everyone."

This approach helped Jackie learn social skills in a supportive way without feeling criticized. For Shantel, it was fulfilling to see her daughter grow in confidence and consideration for others.

The Power of Words and Encouragement: Ephesians 4:29 (NIV) says "Do not let any unwholesome talk come out of your mouths, but only what helps build others up according to their needs, that it may benefit those who listen." Shantel's positive reinforcement mirrors the biblical principle of using words to encourage and build others up rather than tear them down.

KEY TAKEAWAYS

★ **Teachable Moments:** Positive discipline transforms missteps into opportunities for growth, teaching children responsibility, accountability, and better decision-making.

★ **Strengthening Bonds:** When discipline is rooted in respect and collaboration, it fosters trust and mutual understanding, deepening the parent-child relationship.

★ **Benefits for Mothers:** For mothers, positive discipline allows them to guide and teach their children without the stress and tension of constant conflict. It promotes a nurturing and cooperative relationship, creating an environment where mother and child feel respected and valued. Mothers can help their children grow into thoughtful, responsible, and emotionally intelligent individuals by focusing on understanding, encouragement, and gentle correction.

★ **Benefits for Children:** Positive discipline equips children with essential life skills, such as emotional regulation, problem-solving, and empathy. They learn to see mistakes as opportunities for growth rather than sources of shame, which helps build their confidence and resilience.

REFLECTIVE QUESTIONS

★   Am I disciplining my child in a way that reflects God's love and grace?

_____

_____

_____

_____

_____

_____

_____

_____

_____

★   How can I turn moments of discipline into teaching opportunities?

_____

_____

_____

_____

_____

_____

_____

_____

★ Do I model the behavior I want my child to emulate?

_____

_____

_____

_____

_____

_____

_____

_____

_____

Affirmations

I guide my child with love, not fear.

Discipline is about teaching, not punishing.

I correct behavior while protecting my child's dignity.

I focus on solutions, not shame.

I stay calm and clear, even in moments of frustration.

My tone is firm but filled with respect.

I model the self-control I want my child to learn.

Every challenge is an opportunity to teach life skills.

I separate my child's behavior from their worth.

I lead with empathy so my child feels heard and understood.

I choose discipline that builds character and responsibility.

I give consequences that teach, not harm.

I am consistent so my child feels secure in my guidance.

I discipline with the long-term goal of raising a kind, capable adult.

My love is the foundation of every boundary I set.

BIBLE VERSES

★   "Whoever spares the rod hates their children, but the one who loves their children is careful to discipline them." Proverbs 13:24 (NIV)

★   "Fathers, do not exasperate your children; instead, bring them up in the training and instruction of the Lord." Ephesians 6:4 (NIV)

★   "Because the Lord disciplines the one he loves, and he chastens everyone he accepts as his son." Hebrews 12:6 (NIV)

★   "Fathers, do not embitter your children, or they will become discouraged." Colossians 3:21 (NIV)

PRAYER

Heavenly Father,

I come to You seeking wisdom and guidance as I strive to discipline my children in a way that reflects Your grace and love. Teach me to correct with patience and to guide with understanding. Please help me see discipline not as a means to control but as an opportunity to teach and nurture their hearts.

Give me the strength to remain calm when I feel frustrated and the clarity to address behaviors constructively. Please help me focus on shaping their character and guiding them toward better choices rather than reacting out of anger or disappointment. Show me how to balance firmness with compassion so my children learn boundaries while feeling secure in my love. Teach me to guide them toward righteousness without anger or frustration. May my corrections be rooted in Your truth and lead them closer to You.

When I struggle to find the right words, fill my heart with Your wisdom and let my actions reflect Your teachings. Lord, help me to discipline my child in love and patience. Please help me to model accountability and forgiveness so they understand the importance of these values in their own lives. May my discipline encourage growth, build trust, and point them to Your truth.

In Jesus' name, Amen.

Chapter 7

Foster Emotional Intelligence

I struggled to foster emotional intelligence when my oldest child was a toddler because it was so much easier for me to make decisions for her. I wanted to protect her from the hurt, pain, and failure I experienced. In the moment, it felt like the right thing to do was to shield her from difficult situations to keep her safe. I was so focused on ensuring she didn't experience disappointment or frustration that I overlooked the value of letting her face emotions. Stepping in deprived her of the opportunity to learn how to handle her emotions, face challenges, and develop resilience. I wanted to protect her, and that will never change, but I've learned that sometimes, letting her experience setbacks is the best way to help her grow emotionally.

When lack of security surfaced, forcing me to feel as if I needed to protect her, I turned to God asking for the wisdom to guide her through, rather than around, life's challenges. My instinct as a mother was to protect her from pain, disappointment, and struggle, but I reminded myself that true strength came from learning how to navigate hardships, not avoid them. In those moments, I prayed, "Lord, help me trust You with my child. Give me discernment to know when to step in and when to let her grow."

I turned to scriptures, like Isaiah 41:10 (NIV), where God says, "So do not fear, for I am with you." This reminded me that as He walked with me through my struggles, He would also walk with my child. Instead of fixing everything for her, I asked God to help me be a safe space where she could process her emotions, teaching her how to turn to Him in times of trouble. I reminded her that feelings, whether fear, sadness, or frustration, were not weaknesses but opportunities to grow in faith and resilience. By trusting God with my child's journey, I learned to step back, allowing Him to shape her heart while I offered love, guidance, and prayer every step of the way.

Promoting emotional intelligence in children is one of the most profound gifts a mother can give. By teaching emotional awareness and empathy, mothers help their children build stronger relationships, navigate challenges, and respond to the world with kindness and resilience. This foundational skill impacts their interactions with others, their ability to solve problems, and their emotional well-being throughout life. Modeling these behaviors in everyday life further reinforces their importance. It's through our own actions and choices that we impart these lessons most effectively. When my children see me handling my emotions with grace, they begin to understand how to regulate their own.

Promoting emotional intelligence aligns with God's design for wisdom, self-control, and compassion in relationships. The Bible teaches that understanding and managing emotions is essential for living a righteous life. Proverbs 16:32 (NIV) states, "Better a patient person than a warrior, one with self-control than one who takes a city." This verse highlights the value of emotional regulation, patience, and wisdom over impulsive reactions. God values our ability to manage our emotions, as it reflects maturity and spiritual growth. As our Heavenly Father, God demonstrates emotional intelligence through His patience, mercy, and righteous anger. His actions show that even in moments of discipline, His heart remains rooted in love and the desire for growth in His children. Teaching children to respond to challenges with wisdom rather than impulsivity reflects God's desire for His people to be emotionally mature and spiritually grounded. Mothers can follow this example by helping their children recognize, understand, and manage their emotions healthily.

Jesus also exemplified emotional intelligence in His interactions with others. He showed deep empathy and understanding of people's emotions and responded with love and wisdom. In John 11:35 (NIV), "Jesus wept" at Lazarus' death, showing He fully experienced and expressed emotions while comforting those grieving. He displayed righteous anger when clearing the temple (Matthew 21:12-13 NIV), demonstrating that emotions can serve a higher purpose when used wisely. As single mothers we can emulate Jesus by helping their children navigate their emotions gracefully—teaching them to express feelings appropriately, empathize with others, and seek God in times of distress.

Let's look at how practicing emotional intelligence benefits mothers and children.

Helping a Child Navigate Big Emotions:

Mya has an 8-year-old son, Joshua, who often struggles with frustration and anger when things don't go his way. Joshua would get upset if he lost when playing board games with friends, sometimes even yelling or leaving the room. Mya realized this was a perfect opportunity to teach Joshua about recognizing and managing his emotions.

One evening, after a tough game night, Mya sat down with Joshua to discuss what happened. She explained that it's normal to feel upset or disappointed, but it's important to express those feelings in a way that doesn't hurt others or himself. Together, they created a "calm-down plan" that Joshua could use whenever he felt overwhelmed. They practiced taking deep breaths, counting to ten, and saying, "I feel frustrated because I wanted to win." Mya also modeled this behavior during stressful moments, saying, "I'm feeling frustrated right now, so I'm going to take a few deep breaths to calm down."

Over time, Joshua began using the strategies they practiced. During the next game night, when he started to feel frustrated, he paused, took a few deep breaths, and said, "I feel upset, but I'm okay." His friends noticed the change, and the game continued peacefully. Mya was proud of Joshua for learning to manage his emotions and grateful for the closer bond they developed by working through the challenge together. This experience taught Joshua that emotions are normal and manageable and gave him tools to use in other areas of his life.

Control our Emotions: Ephesians 4:26 (NIV) says, "In your anger do not sin: Do not let the sun go down while you are still angry," which emphasizes not letting negative emotions dictate our actions. Joshua's pause and deep breaths before reacting reflect this Biblical principle of emotional regulation.

Encouraging Empathy and Understanding:

Linda whose 9-year-old daughter, Nova, often struggled to see things from others' perspectives. Nova sometimes argued with her friends, insisting she was always right without considering their feelings. Linda wanted to help Nova develop empathy and better interpersonal skills.

One day, after Nova argued with her best friend, Linda used the situation as a teachable moment. She asked Sophie to describe how her friend might have felt during the disagreement. At first, Nova resisted, focusing only on her perspective. But with gentle encouragement, Linda guided her to think about her friend's feelings by asking questions like, "How do you think she felt when you said that?" and "What would you feel if the roles were reversed?"

Linda also shared stories from her own life, recounting times when she had to step back and consider someone else's point of view. To reinforce the lesson, Linda suggested they do a small act of kindness together, like writing a note to Nova's friend to apologize and make amends. Nova agreed, and her friend appreciated the gesture.

Over time, Linda noticed a positive change in Nova. She asked questions like, "Do you think that hurt their feelings?" and "How can I improve this?" Nova's relationships with her friends improved, and she became more thoughtful and considerate. Linda felt proud of Nova's growth and grateful she could guide her daughter toward greater empathy and understanding.

Empathy and Consideration for Others: Nova's development of empathy, asking how her actions may affect others, aligns with the principle of loving others as we love ourselves, as seen in Matthew 7:12 (NIV) "So in everything, do to others what you would have them do to you, for this sums up the Law and the Prophets." This verse encourages thoughtful consideration of others' feelings and treating them with kindness, which reflects how Nova's character is growing in this passage.

KEY TAKEAWAYS

★   **Teaching Emotional Regulation:** Helping children recognize and manage their emotions empowers them to handle challenges calmly and constructively. This skill builds resilience and fosters stronger relationships.

★   **Developing Empathy:** Encouraging children to consider others' feelings nurtures compassion and understanding, which is essential for building meaningful connections.

★   **Benefits for Mothers:** When mothers invest in fostering emotional intelligence in their children, they create an environment of open communication, trust, and mutual respect. It joys mothers to watch their children grow into kind, thoughtful, and emotionally mature individuals.

★   **Benefits for Children:** Children with emotional awareness and empathy are better prepared to navigate conflicts, cope with stress, and build healthy relationships.

★   By modeling emotional intelligence in your life by representing patience, empathy, and the ability to manage emotions, you teach your child these vital skills through example. The effort you put into nurturing your child's emotional growth strengthens their character and deepens the bond between you and your child, laying the foundation for a lifetime of meaningful connections and emotional well-being.

REFLECTIVE QUESTIONS

★ Do I validate my child's emotions, even when I don't agree with their reactions?

_____

_____

_____

_____

_____

_____

_____

★ How can I help my child manage big emotions in healthy ways?

_____

_____

_____

_____

_____

_____

_____

_____

_____

★ Am I modeling empathy and understanding in my interactions?

_____

_____

_____

_____

_____

_____

_____

_____

_____

AFFIRMATIONS

I help my child name and understand their feelings without judgment.

I teach my child that all emotions are valid, but not all actions are acceptable.

I guide my child to express themselves in healthy and respectful ways.

I model self-awareness so my child learns to notice their own emotions.

I encourage my child to pause and reflect before reacting.

I use challenges as opportunities to teach empathy and compassion.

I show my child how to repair relationships after conflict.

I validate my child's feelings while holding them accountable for their actions.

I help my child see that mistakes are lessons, not labels.

I practice patience so my child feels safe to share openly with me.

I use discipline to teach self-control, not to create fear.

I encourage my child to listen to their inner voice with kindness.

I model how to communicate needs without hurting others.

I guide my child toward solutions that honor both their feelings and boundaries.

I raise my child to be emotionally aware, resilient, and compassionate.

BIBLE VERSES

★ "A hot-tempered person stirs up conflict, but the one who is patient calms a quarrel." Proverbs 15:18 (NIV)

★ "But the fruit of the Spirit is love, joy, peace, forbearance, kindness, goodness, faithfulness, gentleness, and self-control." Galatians 5:22-23 (NIV)

★ "Rejoice with those who rejoice; mourn with those who mourn." Romans 12:15 (NIV)

★ "Everyone should be quick to listen, slow to speak, and slow to become angry." James 1:19 (NIV)

PRAYER

Heavenly Father,

Grant me the words to comfort and encourage them when they struggle with big feelings. Give me insight into recognizing their emotional needs and the tools to help them navigate challenges confidently and gracefully. Help me to create a safe and open environment where they feel valued and understood. May they grow in understanding their feelings and showing compassion to others. Grant me the grace to be patient as they learn and mature.

May I also grow in my emotional awareness, leaning on Your strength during moments of frustration or doubt. Fill my heart with compassion and wisdom so that I can be the loving guide my children need as they learn to manage their emotions and build meaningful relationships.

Thank You for the gift of motherhood and for entrusting me with these precious souls. Thank you for equipping me with the patience and love to foster emotional growth in their hearts.

In Jesus' name, Amen.

Chapter 8

Spend Quality Time Together

As a single mother, I constantly found myself torn between exhaustion and guilt when it came to spending time with my children. I wanted to be present, but the truth was, I was drained mentally, emotionally, and physically. Between work, household responsibilities, and just trying to hold everything together, I craved even a moment to myself. The constant noise, demands, and overstimulation left me completely overwhelmed; when my children were incredibly disobedient, it became even more challenging. Instead of facing endless battles, I found myself avoiding interactions with my children, not because I didn't love them, but because I felt like I had nothing left to give. It felt like I was caught in a cycle of giving and giving until I was empty, and I wondered if I was doing enough for them, despite my best efforts. The weight of motherhood as a single parent sometimes felt unbearable, and there were moments when I felt like I was falling short. In these times, it was important for me to remember that needing time for myself didn't make me a bad mother. It made me human.

When I felt overstimulated, I learned to create small moments of connection with God, even in the chaos. I whispered prayers, asking for patience, peace and strength, knowing He heard me even in exhaustion. Sometimes, I stole a few minutes to read a Bible verse or listen to worship music while doing chores, letting His presence wash over me. I found that these moments, no matter how small, were enough to refresh my spirit and remind me that I didn't have to do it all alone. When I felt overwhelmed by my child's disobedience, I reminded myself that just as God extended grace to me, I had to extend it to my child. And when I felt like I had nothing left, I surrendered it all to Him, trusting that He would renew my strength.

Spending quality time with your child is one of the most impactful ways to strengthen your relationship and promote their emotional well-being. By engaging in activities your child enjoys and prioritizing one-on-one moments, you create a safe space to express themselves, feel valued, and know they are loved. These shared moments build trust, deepen your connection, and create cherished memories that stay with both of you for a lifetime. Children thrive on undivided attention, and these moments show them that they are important to you, even when life is chaotic.

Jesus spent quality time with His Father through prayer, solitude, and devotion. Throughout His ministry, Jesus often withdrew to quiet places to communicate with God, seeking guidance, strength, and connection. This intimate relationship was built on love, trust, and constant communication, showing their deep bond. By prioritizing time with God, Jesus demonstrated the importance of spiritual closeness and reliance on the Father's wisdom. In those quiet moments, Jesus found the peace and strength to continue His mission, and this serves as a model for me as a parent. I've learned that by nurturing my relationship with God, I am better equipped to nurture my relationship with my children.

As single mothers we can model this behavior by intentionally spending quality time with their children, just as Jesus did with God. Setting aside moments for meaningful conversations, shared activities, and spiritual growth fosters a strong and loving relationship. Whether through prayer, reading together, or simply being present, parents can teach their children the value of connection, trust, and love. By mirroring Jesus' relationship with God, families can build deeper bonds and nurture a sense of faith and unity.

Let's look at examples of how spending quality time together benefits mothers and children.

Strengthening Emotional Connection Through Shared Hobbies:

Danielle, who has a 10-year-old son, Renald. Renald loves soccer, but Danielle was never particularly interested in sports. She usually stayed on the sidelines during his practices and games, cheering him on but never engaging beyond that. One day, Danielle realized that while she was supporting Renald by being present, she wasn't truly connecting with him in an area that brought him joy. She decided to make a change.

Danielle began asking Renald about his favorite players and games and even started playing soccer in the backyard after school. Although she wasn't skilled at the game, Renald loved teaching her the basics, laughing when she missed a kick, and cheering when she scored a goal. Over time, these casual backyard games became a daily tradition they both looked forward to. Danielle noticed that Renald opened up more about his day during these moments. He shared his school struggles, dreams of becoming a professional player, and worries about an upcoming test.

Danielle and Renald's bond grew stronger through their shared love of soccer. Renald's felt valued because his mom took the time to engage in an activity he loved, even though it wasn't her comfort zone. Danielle discovered that the time spent playing soccer wasn't just about the game but about creating a space where Renald felt safe and loved. This experience taught Danielle that spending quality time in her child's world deepened their connection and gave her insight into his thoughts and feelings.

God's Desire for Relationship: Just as Danielle's presence helped Renald feel valued, God desires closeness with His children and calls mothers to reflect His love. As shown in Deuteronomy 6:6-7 (NIV) "These commandments that I give you today are to be on your hearts. Impress them on your children. Talk about them when you sit at home, walk along the road, lie down, and get up." Danielle's intentional efforts to engage with Renald demonstrate the biblical principle that love is shown through action and presence. Just as God is present in our lives, mothers can reflect His love by actively engaging in their children's world.

Prioritizing One-on-One Time Amidst a Busy Schedule:

Breyanna has three children of different ages. With so many responsibilities and activities, Breyanna often felt stretched thin and struggled to spend individual time with each child. Her middle child, Erma, began acting out at school, and Breyanna realized that Erma might be feeling overlooked.

To address this, Breyanna decided to set aside regular one-on-one time with each of her children. For Erma, they began a tradition of "Friday night talks," where they would grab ice cream and chat about anything on Erma's mind. At first, their conversations were lighthearted, and Erma would talk about her favorite books or funny moments at school. But over time, Erma began sharing deeper feelings, such as her frustration about being stuck in the middle sibling role and her struggles with friendships.

Breyanna listened attentively without judgment and used these moments to affirm Erma's feelings and offer guidance. Over time, Erma's behavior improved, and her relationship with Breyanna grew stronger. Erma felt seen and heard, knowing her mom valued their time together. Breyanna, in turn, realized how much she cherished these moments and how vital it was to make space for each child individually.

Individual Time & Nurturing Relationships: Breyanna recognizes the value of intentional time with each child, which aligns with God's desire for parents to nurture and invest in their children's hearts. Deuteronomy 6:6-7 (NIV) states "These commandments that I give you today are to be on your hearts. Impress them on your children. Talk about them when you sit at home, walk along the road, lie down, and get up." Breyanna and Erma's example highlights the power of intentional parenting, love, and wisdom, mirroring how God listens, guides, and strengthens His relationship with us.

KEY TAKEAWAYS

★ **Connection Through Shared Activities:** When you join your child in an activity they enjoy, it communicates that their interests matter to you. These moments often lead to deeper conversations and strengthen emotional bonds.

★ **Individualized Attention:** Setting aside dedicated one-on-one time with your child helps them feel valued and loved. It also creates opportunities for deeper understanding and open communication.

★ **Benefits for Mothers:** For mothers, these moments provide insight into their child's world, allowing them to guide, support, and celebrate their child meaningfully.

★ **Benefits to Children:** Spending quality time together builds trust, strengthens emotional bonds, and fosters a sense of security in your child. These shared experiences teach them the importance of relationships and create lasting memories they will carry into adulthood.

REFLECTIVE QUESTIONS

★   How can I make quality time with my child a daily priority?

_____

_____

_____

_____

_____

_____

_____

_____

★   What activities can we do together that will foster our relationship?

_____

_____

_____

_____

_____

_____

_____

★   Am I fully present during the time I spend with my child?

_____

_____

_____

_____

_____

_____

_____

_____

_____

_____

AFFIRMATIONS

I make time each day to truly connect with my child.

I am fully present when I am with my child.

Our moments together are just as important as our responsibilities.

I choose connection over distraction.

I listen deeply and engage fully during our time together.

I create memories that my child will carry in their heart forever.

Even small moments of connection make a big impact.

I value our laughter, conversations, and shared experiences.

I put away distractions so my child knows they matter most.

I show my love through my time, attention, and presence.

I make space for fun, play, and creativity with my child.

I nurture our bond through meaningful activities and shared joy.

I savor the present moment with my child without rushing.

Our time together builds trust, love, and understanding.

I treasure every opportunity to grow closer to my child.

BIBLE VERSES

★ "There is a time for everything and a season for every activity under the heavens." Ecclesiastes 3:1 (NIV)

★ "Children are a heritage from the Lord, offspring a reward from him." Psalms 127:3 (NIV)

★ "Love is patient, love is kind. It does not envy, it does not boast, it is not proud... It always protects, always trusts, always hopes, always perseveres.1 Corinthians 13:4-7 (NIV)

★ "A cheerful heart is good medicine, but a crushed spirit dries up the bones." Proverbs 17:22 (NIV)

PRAYER

Heavenly Father,

Thank You for my children's incredible gift and the opportunity to spend precious moments with them. Lord, thank You for the gift of time with my children. Help me to prioritize our time together and to be fully present in those moments. Teach me to engage with their hearts, to listen without distraction, and to make memories that will strengthen our relationship. Help me to be present and intentional in our moments together. May our time be filled with joy, love, and opportunities to grow closer to each other and You.

Give me the creativity and patience to find activities that bring joy to their hearts. Help me to balance life's demands so that my children never feel overlooked or undervalued. Let my time with them reflect Your love, building a foundation of trust, connection, and understanding. When I feel tired or overwhelmed, remind me of these moments' importance and lasting impact. Fill my heart with gratitude for these opportunities to grow closer to my children and to nurture their spirits. May our time together bring glory to You and deepen our family's bond.

In Jesus' name, Amen.

CHAPTER 9
Consistency

As a single mother, I wanted to be consistent with my children, but oftentimes, exhaustion, depression, and lack of motivation made it incredibly difficult to do so. Some days, I had the energy to set routines, enforce boundaries, and be fully engaged, but other days, I was just trying to survive. The constant demands of my children often wore me down, and when depression crept in, even the most minor tasks felt overwhelming. It was hard to maintain a routine when my own emotional and physical was inconsistent at best. When I was running on empty, it was hard to follow through. One day, I had the patience to guide my child with love; the next, I was too drained to correct behavior and let things slide. I wished I could be perfect every day, but I fell short more often than I'd like to admit. As a result, my inconsistent behavior led to guilt, frustration, and self-doubt, leaving me feeling as if I was failing.

When a pattern of inconsistency presented itself, I reminded myself that His grace covered my shortcomings. I took a deep breath and prayed, asking Him to strengthen me where I felt weak and guide me where I felt lost. I turned to Scripture, finding comfort in verses like "My grace is sufficient for you, for my power is made perfect in weakness." 2 Corinthians 12:9 (ESV). This reminder that God's grace was sufficient in my weakest moments gave me peace and reassured me that I didn't have to be perfect. I reminded myself that I wasn't parenting alone and that God was with me, filling the gaps where I fell short. Instead of dwelling in guilt, I surrendered my struggles to Him, asking for wisdom and renewal. I also tried to speak life over myself, saying, "I am not a failure; I am a mother covered by grace." These affirmations helped me shift my focus from what I could not do to what God was doing through me. And when I didn't know what else to do, I simply sat in His presence, trusting that He would restore me, one moment at a time.

Consistency is one of the most potent tools a mother can use to create an environment of trust, security, and clear expectations. Consistent in your words and actions helps your child feel more secure, knowing what to expect from you and what is expected of them. This sense of stability is vital for their emotional well-being and ability to navigate challenges. When children know what to expect from their parents, it creates a safe space for them to thrive. Consistency fosters a safe environment where children feel secure enough to explore, make mistakes, and grow. It also teaches them the value of follow-through, responsibility, and accountability, which are crucial life skills.

Jesus exemplified consistency in His teachings, actions, and love. He remained steadfast in His mission, showing compassion to all, praying regularly, and upholding truth despite adversity. His unwavering commitment to God's will is a model of faithfulness, demonstrating that proper consistency is rooted in love, humility, and righteousness. He didn't change based on the circumstances around Him. His love and commitment to His mission remained the same regardless of how He was treated or the difficulties He faced.

God, as the ultimate example of consistency, remains unchanging in His character, promises, and love for humanity. His faithfulness endures through all circumstances, offering guidance, grace, and justice without fail. Parents can model this consistency by being dependable in their words and actions and nurturing their children with love, discipline, and faith, just as God does with His children.

Let's look at examples of how consistency benefits both mothers and children.

Creating Consistent Routines for Emotional Security:

Katherine, who has a 6-year-old son, Brayden. Katherine noticed that Brayden tended to get anxious about the school day ahead. Sometimes, he would throw tantrums or refuse to get dressed, and Katherine wasn't sure how to address the behavior. It was difficult for

Brayden to transition from the calm of home to the demands of school, and Katherine realized that the inconsistency in their morning routine was contributing to his anxiety.

Katherine implemented a consistent morning routine to provide Brayden with more emotional security. Each day, they followed the same sequence: wake up at the same time, have breakfast, get dressed, pack the school bag, and then have a few minutes of quiet playtime or reading before leaving for school. Katherine explained the new routine to Brayden, assuring him that following it would help him feel more in control and less anxious.

At first, Brayden resisted the change, but Katherine stuck to the routine every day, even when Brayden was upset or wanted to skip steps. Over time, Brayden began to feel more secure, knowing what to expect each morning. He became more independent in getting dressed and preparing for school, and his anxiety decreased because the routine provided him with the stability he needed. The consistency in the morning routine helped Brayden feel more in control of his day and built trust between him and Katherine. He knew she would be there to guide him through the day, and that made him feel safe.

This experience taught Katherine the power of consistency in providing emotional security. By committing to a consistent routine, Katherine helped Brayden develop a sense of control and trust in his environment, reducing his anxiety and setting him up for success daily.

Building Responsibility: The Bible emphasizes the importance of creating a nurturing and stable environment for children. Isaiah 54:13 (NIV) states "All your children will be taught by the Lord, and great will be their peace." Katherine's efforts in maintaining a routine bring peace and security to Brayden's life, much like the biblical principle of raising children in an environment that fosters well-being.

Raising Children with Stability and Wisdom

Lisa, who has a 9-year-old daughter, Ava. Ava had been testing boundaries when it came to screen time. She would often ignore the agreed-upon time limits for TV and video games, and when Lisa would remind her of the rules, Ava would argue, often in an attempt to push for more time. Lisa was initially inconsistent in enforcing the rules because she didn't want to cause conflict or disrupt Ava's enjoyment. Sometimes, she would let Ava have more screen time, especially if she was tired or overwhelmed from work.

However, Lisa soon realized that her inconsistent enforcement of screen time rules was confusing for Ava. Sometimes, Ava would get more screen time and sometimes less, and this inconsistency made Ava feel uncertain about what was expected of her. It also resulted in more frequent arguments and increased resistance.

To resolve this, Lisa decided to be more consistent with the rules. She communicated with Ava about the screen time limits and the consequences for not following the rules. She also set clear expectations, telling Ava exactly how much screen time she would get each day and when it would end. On days when Ava tried to push the limits, Lisa calmly reminded her of the agreement and followed through with the established consequences, whether turning off the screen or limiting her screen time the following day.

At first, Ava showed some resistance, but as Lisa stuck to the rules consistently, Ava began to understand that the limits were non-negotiable. Over time, Ava learned to manage her screen time better, and Lisa no longer had to constantly remind her. Ava knew that if she followed the rules, she would get the allotted screen time, and if she didn't, there would be consequences. This consistency helped Ava develop responsibility and respect for the boundaries set, strengthening her ability to manage her time and reinforcing the importance of following through with commitments and respecting limits.

Lisa's commitment to consistency in discipline helped foster trust in their relationship and taught Ava the value of responsibility, clear expectations, and accountability. Through consistency, Lisa could guide Ava toward making better choices without constant reminders or power struggles.

The Importance of Consistent Discipline: Lisa's commitment to consistency in discipline aligns with Proverbs 13:24 (NIV) states "Whoever spares the rod hates their children, but the one who loves their children is careful to discipline them." This verse emphasizes that loving discipline is essential for a child's growth. Lisa's consistency reflects love, as it helps Ava understand boundaries and responsibility.

KEY TAKEAWAYS

★ **Benefits for Mothers:** Your child learns what to expect when you are consistent with routines and rules, fostering stability. It also teaches them essential life skills, such as time management, responsibility, and the value of follow-through.

★ **Benefits for Children:** When children experience consistency from their mothers, they feel more secure and can better focus on learning, growing, and making positive decisions. They learn to trust that their mothers will be there to guide them and that promises and consequences are meaningful and reliable. This sense of predictability gives them the confidence to explore the world, knowing that some boundaries and structures keep them safe and secure.

REFLECTIVE QUESTIONS

★ Do my actions align with the rules and expectations I set for my child?

_____

_____

_____

_____

_____

_____

_____

_____

★ How can I improve consistency in enforcing boundaries?

_____

_____

_____

_____

_____

_____

_____

_____

★   Am I reliable in keeping promises to my child?

_____

_____

_____

_____

_____

_____

_____

_____

AFFIRMATION

My consistency helps my child feel safe and secure.

I follow through on my words with actions my child can trust.

I provide steady guidance so my child knows what to expect.

I am reliable in both my love and my boundaries.

Consistency in discipline teaches my child responsibility and respect.

I show up for my child the same way every day—with love and intention.

I keep my promises to build trust with my child.

I model reliability so my child learns to be dependable.

I am patient and steady, even when progress feels slow.

Consistency in routines gives my child a strong foundation.

I set clear expectations and uphold them with kindness.

I do not waver in my commitment to my child's growth and well-being.

I guide my child with the same love in both good and challenging moments.

Consistency in my actions shows my child that they can count on me.

I create stability in our home through my dependable presence and care.

BIBLE VERSES

★ "Let your 'Yes' be yes, and your 'No,' no, or you will be condemned." James 5:12 (NIV)

★ "All you need to say is simply 'Yes' or 'No'; anything beyond this comes from the evil one." Matthew 5:37 (NIV)

★ "Jesus Christ is the same yesterday and today and forever." Hebrews 13:8 (NIV)

★ "For the Spirit God gave us does not make us timid, but gives us power, love, and self-discipline." 2 Timothy 1:7 (NIV)

PRAYER

Heavenly Father,

Thank You for being the ultimate example of consistency and faithfulness in my life. Help me, Lord, to model this same steadiness for my children. Grant me the strength and discipline to align my words with my actions and follow through with promises and consequences.

When life feels overwhelming, it reminds me of the importance of consistency in my children's lives. Teach me to build routines that foster security and trust and help me to apply boundaries with fairness and love. May my actions reflect Your unwavering love and dependability.

I ask for wisdom in moments when consistency feels challenging. Guide me to make decisions that honor You and benefit my children. Let my efforts to be steady and reliable lead them to feel safe and secure, knowing they can trust in my word and Your promises.

Thank You for entrusting me with the gift of motherhood. May my commitment to consistency bring glory to You and bless my children with a foundation of trust and stability.

In Jesus' name, Amen.

CHAPTER 10
Celebrate Effort, Not Just Results

As a single mother, I sometimes struggled to celebrate my oldest child's effort instead of just the results, not because I didn't want to, but because I was never taught how. I found myself emulating what I was taught or what I saw other parents do, praising success but overlooking the small steps it took to get there. As a child, my effort wasn't recognized but my success was praised. After working in family therapy for a while, I was able to recognize and remember how my parents' actions led me to feel as a child. Empathy helped me shift my mindset to remind myself that growth came from the process, not just the outcome. I wanted my children to know that perseverance, resilience, and determination mattered as much, if not more, than the final result.

When I struggled to celebrate results instead of effort and fell into old patterns, I asked God to renew my perspective. I asked Him for wisdom to break generational habits and for the grace to encourage my children in a way that built confidence, not pressure. I knew that their worth was not determined by perfection, but by their persistence and willingness to grow. When I felt myself slipping into old ways, I paused and thanked God for every step my children took, learning to celebrate the process rather than just the achievement. Through prayer and reflection, I reminded myself to intentionally recognize and affirm my children just as God was patient with my growth. I pray, "Lord, help me see my child the way You see me, not for perfection, but for growth, persistence, and heart." I remind myself that God doesn't just reward the outcome; He honors the journey. Verses like Colossians

3:23 (NIV), which says, "Whatever you do, work at it with all your heart, as working for the Lord," remind me that effort is valuable in His eyes. Every attempt, whether successful or not, is a reflection of my child's growth and commitment to trying.

By celebrating effort and progress, you nurture your child's resilience, determination, and growth mindset rather than simply focusing on results. This approach helps them understand that success is a journey, not a destination, and that the effort they put into learning and growing is far more critical than any immediate outcome. When I emphasized their efforts, I helped my children develop the confidence and perseverance they needed to tackle life's challenges, knowing that every step forward, no matter how small, was a victory. It also helped reduce their fear of failure, knowing that failure was not something to avoid, but an integral part of learning and growing. As a mother, my support and encouragement in these moments helped my child develop the confidence and perseverance they needed to tackle life's challenges, knowing that every step forward, no matter how small, was a victory.

In the Bible, God and Jesus model the importance of celebrating efforts, not just results, by valuing faithfulness, perseverance, and a willing heart. God looks at the heart rather than mere achievements, as seen when He chose David as king, not for his outward stature but for his character (1 Samuel 16:7 NIV). God saw the effort and sincerity of David's heart, not just his accomplishments. Similarly, Jesus affirms this principle in the Parable of the Widow's Offering (Mark 12:41-44 NIV). He praises a poor widow who gave a small amount because she gave all she had, highlighting that effort and sacrifice matter more than quantity. This story teaches that what we give, regardless of how small it may seem, is valued by God when it comes from the heart. In the Parable of the Talents (Matthew 25:21), the master commends the faithful servants for their gain and diligence, saying, "Well done, good and faithful servant." Likewise, God encourages persistence in doing good (Galatians 6:9) and celebrates progress, knowing that growth takes time. This teaches parents to affirm their children's efforts, resilience, and intentions rather than solely focusing on the outcome, fostering confidence, motivation, and a heart willing to try.

Let's look at some examples of how celebrating effort and not just results benefits both mothers and children.

Academic Struggles and Personal Growth:

Keyara, whose daughter, Kai, has always struggled with math. Early in Kai's academic career, she often brought home grades that didn't reflect her time and energy studying. Kai would usually be discouraged and upset with herself, feeling like she would never get better. Instead of focusing on the grade, Keyara praised Kai's consistent effort, emphasizing that she was learning more than the numbers on the paper showed.

One evening, after Kai received another low grade on a math test, Keyara sat down to review her work. They worked through the problems together, discussing where things went wrong, and Keyara encouraged Kai to keep practicing, reminding her that learning is a process and that improvement often takes time. Keisha said, "I'm proud of how hard you worked on this, even though the results don't reflect it. Each time you try, you're getting one step closer to understanding it better."

As a result of this approach, Kai began to understand that effort was valuable, not just the grades. Over the next few months, Kai started to approach math with a new attitude, no longer afraid of mistakes but excited to learn from them. Eventually, she did improve her math skills, but the most crucial change was the shift in her mindset. She no longer feared challenges or failure because she understood that consistent effort and perseverance would lead to growth, even if the results weren't immediate.

The Value of Effort and Perseverance: Kai's understanding that effort itself is valuable, not just the results, aligns with Galatians 6:9 (NIV) "Let us not become weary in doing good, for at the proper time we will reap a harvest if we do not give up." This verse encourages persistence and highlights that consistent effort, even in the face of challenges, will eventually lead to positive outcomes. Kai's shift in mindset reflects the biblical principle that hard work and perseverance will yield growth, even when immediate results are not evident.

Sports and Building Confidence:

Esther is a mother of an 8-year-old boy named Levi, who loves playing soccer. Levi's team often competes in local leagues, and while he loves the game, he usually feels discouraged when his team loses or when he misses an important goal. Initially, Esther was concerned because Levi would get down on himself and stop enjoying the game altogether. Instead of emphasizing the game's outcome, she focused on the effort and improvement he showed during practice and in the game itself.

One afternoon, after a particularly tough match where Levi missed several opportunities to score, Esther took him aside. She said, "I saw you running hard and trying to make those passes, and that's what matters most to me. You gave it your all, which we should be proud of. You're improving with every game." Esther then worked with Levi on the areas he wanted to improve, such as his footwork and decision-making during plays, reinforcing that his focus should be on getting better, not just winning.

Over time, Levi's mindset shifted. He started enjoying soccer because of the game's love, not just the victories. He became more willing to take risks on the field, knowing that it was okay to make mistakes as long as he gave his best effort. His resilience grew, and he started seeing mistakes as opportunities to improve, which helped him become a more confident and capable player over time. Esther's encouragement was crucial in helping him develop a strong foundation of perseverance, both on and off the field.

Perseverance and Endurance: One biblical verse that exemplifies this principle is Romans 5:3-4 (NIV) "Not only so, but we also glory in our sufferings, because we know that suffering produces perseverance; perseverance, character; and character, hope." Levi's shift in mindset reflects this principle, where his willingness to take risks and view mistakes as opportunities to improve shows the development of perseverance. Just as this passage teaches that challenges and struggles build perseverance, Levi's experiences on the soccer field, with Esther's encouragement, reflect the growth process that leads to stronger resilience and character.

KEY TAKEAWAYS

★ **Focusing on Effort and Progress:** Praise your child's consistent effort and growth, rather than just the final outcome, to encourage a growth mindset and resilience.

★ **Encouraging Resilience Through Challenges:** Emphasize the importance of learning from mistakes and setbacks, helping children view challenges as opportunities for improvement.

★ **Benefits for Mothers:** Mothers can help cultivate their children's resilience and perseverance, creating a positive environment where effort is valued over perfection.

★ **Benefits to Children:** Children develop a growth mindset, learn to embrace mistakes, and become more confident, motivated, and resilient in facing challenges.

REFLECTIVE QUESTIONS

★ Do I acknowledge and praise my child's efforts as much as their achievements?

_____

_____

_____

_____

_____

_____

_____

★ How can I encourage a growth mindset in my child?

_____

_____

_____

_____

_____

_____

_____

_____

★ Am I helping my child see challenges as opportunities to grow?

_____

_____

_____

_____

_____

_____

_____

_____

AFFIRMATIONS

I praise my child's hard work and dedication, not just their achievements.

I value progress over perfection.

I celebrate the courage it takes for my child to try new things.

Every step forward is a success worth acknowledging.

I teach my child that persistence is more important than instant results.

I honor the lessons learned along the way, not just the finish line.

I remind my child that effort is the foundation of growth.

I focus on my child's determination and problem-solving skills.

I cheer for the attempts, even when the outcome isn't what we hoped.

I encourage my child to see challenges as opportunities to grow.

I praise the process, not just the product.

I help my child find pride in their own progress.

I model perseverance so my child learns the value of not giving up.

I remind my child that learning is a journey, not a race.

I celebrate the heart they put into what they do.

BIBLE VERSES

★ "Whatever you do, work at it with all your heart, as working for the Lord, not for human masters." Colossians 3:23 (NIV)

★ "I can do all this through him who gives me strength." Philippians 4:13 (NIV)

★ "Whatever your hand finds to do, do it with all your might." Ecclesiastes 9:10 (NIV)

★ "Do your best to present yourself to God as one approved, a worker who does not need to be ashamed and who correctly handles the word of truth." 2 Timothy 2:15 (NIV)

Prayer

Heavenly Father,

Thank You for the precious gift of my children. I come before You today with a heart full of gratitude for the opportunity to guide and nurture them. Lord, I know that genuine growth comes not from the perfection of results but from the effort and perseverance we put into our tasks. I ask for Your help in teaching my children the value of effort, progress, and resilience. Help me to recognize their hard work and dedication, even when the results don't reflect their full potential.

I pray that You give me the wisdom to celebrate their efforts, not just their achievements. Help me to see the small victories, the perseverance they show when they try again after a setback, the hard work they put in despite the challenges, and the courage they show in pursuing what seems complicated. May I help them see that every step forward, no matter how small, is a step toward success.

Please give me the patience to guide them through their struggles and the grace to encourage them when they feel discouraged. Let me help them understand that failure is not a sign of defeat but a chance to learn and grow stronger. My words and actions will foster a growth mindset in their hearts so they will learn to embrace challenges with determination and celebrate progress, not just perfection.

I also ask for Your help modeling this mindset. Help me focus on my efforts and growth to show my children that learning and improvement are ongoing journeys for all of us. May I always encourage them to be resilient in the face of adversity, to celebrate every bit of progress, and to trust that their efforts will bear fruit at the right time.

Thank You for the privilege of being their mother. May I be a source of encouragement and strength, guiding them toward a life filled with perseverance, joy, and a deep love of learning.

In Jesus' name, I pray. Amen

Chapter 11
Take Care Of Yourself

As a single mother, I often struggled to take care of myself because I was constantly putting my children's needs first. Their needs came before mine and I felt that responsibility so profoundly that I often neglected my own well-being. There were days when I found myself running on empty, because I had given so much of myself to care for them. When I tried to make time for self-care, I felt guilty, like I was being selfish or not prioritizing what mattered most; my children.

When I felt I was losing myself because I was constantly putting my children's needs first, I sought God by asking Him for the wisdom to find balance. I prayed, "Lord, help me to honor You with my body and mind. Show me how to care for myself without feeling guilty or selfish." I remind myself that God doesn't call me to neglect my health or well-being; instead, He desires me to be whole and serve my children with love and energy. Scriptures like Mark 12:31 (NIV) which says, "Love your neighbor as yourself," help me understand that loving and caring for myself is not selfish but essential to being the best mother I can be.

When guilt arose, I asked God to replace it with peace. I reminded myself that by renewing my own strength, I could be more present, patient and more emotionally available to my children. All while also seeking His guidance in finding small, manageable ways to care for myself through prayer, rest, or nourishing my body. By surrendering my fears and doubts to Him, I trusted He would guide me in creating a healthy balance between caring for my children and nurturing my soul. Taking time to replenish was not a luxury, but a necessity for my own well-being.

Taking care of yourself aligns with God's design for stewardship, balance, and honoring the body and mind He has given us. In 1 Corinthians 6:19-20 (NIV), Paul reminds believers that their bodies are temples of the Holy Spirit, urging them to glorify God in how they care for themselves. This means maintaining physical health, emotional well-being, and spiritual renewal. Just as God rested on the seventh day of creation (Genesis 2:2-3 NIV), He models the importance of rest and self-care. Single mothers, in particular, can draw from this example by prioritizing their well-being, understanding that they cannot pour into their children if they are physically exhausted or spiritually depleted. By practicing self-care, mothers demonstrate to their children the importance of balance, resilience, and trusting God with their burdens.

Jesus also exemplified self-care in His ministry by regularly withdrawing to pray and renew His strength. (Luke 5:16 NIV) states, "But Jesus often withdrew to lonely places and prayed," showing that even the Son of God took time to rest, reflect, and reconnect with His Father. This is a powerful reminder that if Jesus, with His divine mission, took time to care for Himself, then I, as a mother, must also make self-care a priority. As single mothers we can follow this example by setting aside time for personal prayer, reflection, and rejuvenation, ensuring they are mentally, emotionally, and spiritually strong for their families. By caring for themselves, they set a healthy example for their children and position themselves to be more patient, loving, and effective in their parenting. Prioritizing self-care is not selfish; it is a biblical principle that allows individuals to serve God and others more fully.

Single parenting is incredibly demanding and requires constant attention, energy, and emotional investment. As a mother, you may often find yourself putting your child's needs ahead of yours. However, it's essential to remember that to be your child's best version of yourself, you must also prioritize your own physical, emotional, and spiritual well-being. When you care for yourself, you feel better and model healthy habits for your child, teaching them the importance of self-care, boundaries, and balance. This practice instills in them the idea that taking care of oneself is vital for a fulfilling and healthy life. And in doing so, you empower them to recognize the value of nurturing their own well-being as they grow into adults.

Let's examine some examples of how caring for yourself benefits mothers and children.

Physical Well-being and Leading by Example:

Chara has a young child, Zia, and a demanding full-time job. In the past, Chara often found herself neglecting her physical health due to her busy schedule. She would skip meals, stay up late working, and not get enough exercise. As a result, she began to feel constantly fatigued, irritable, and overwhelmed, which, in turn, affected her ability to engage with Zia in a positive, energetic way.

One day, Chara realized her lack of self-care negatively impacted her relationship with her daughter. She couldn't enjoy her time with Zia as much because she constantly felt drained. So, Chara decided to make a change. She prioritized regular exercise, eating healthier meals, and establishing a better sleep routine. Chara also involved Zia by walking together, cooking healthy meals as a team, and making bedtime a relaxing ritual.

By taking care of her physical health, Chara felt more energized and set an example for Zia about the importance of self-care. Zia learned that caring for one's body is essential for feeling good and having the energy to be present for others. This shift improved Chara's well-being and strengthened her relationship with her daughter, as they could now spend more quality time together.

Honoring God with our bodies: As stated in 1 Corinthians 6:19-20 (NIV), "Do you not know that your bodies are temples of the Holy Spirit... Therefore honor God with your bodies." Chara's commitment to self-care reflects this principle, as she honors God by caring for her body. Her example to Zia shows how maintaining physical health can strengthen relationships and be an opportunity to praise God.

Emotional Well-being and Building Healthy Boundaries:

Tatiana is a mother of three children under the age of 10. Tatiana's emotional well-being had been taking a backseat for years as she juggled the constant demands of motherhood, from school runs to meal prep to emotional support for her kids. She often felt overwhelmed, and her emotional resilience started to wear thin. Tatiana repeatedly snapped at her children and felt guilty for not being more patient with them.

After a particularly challenging week, Tatiana stepped back and realized she couldn't rest emotionally. She had no outlet for stress and didn't make time for things that brought her joy. Tatiana decided to carve out time for herself each week, whether that meant reading a book, spending time with friends, or practicing mindfulness. She also learned to set boundaries by communicating her needs to her children in an age-appropriate way. Tatiana explained to her kids that while she loved them dearly, there were moments when she needed quiet time to recharge, and that was important for her emotional health.

As Tatiana began to care for her emotional needs, she noticed a positive change in her interactions with her children. She felt less irritable and more patient, and her children learned the importance of respecting boundaries and understanding that their mom also needed time to take care of herself. Tatiana became a better listener and a more present mother because she learned to tend to her emotional well-being. Her children observed her emotional self-regulation and began understanding the value of managing their emotions, helping them develop emotional intelligence.

Loving others as we love ourselves: Mark 12:31 (NIV) states "Love your neighbor as yourself." Tatiana's focus on her emotional well-being allows her to be a more patient and present mother, demonstrating that taking care of ourselves enables us to better love and serve others. By setting boundaries and modeling emotional self-regulation, she teaches her children the importance of managing their emotions and respecting others' needs.

KEY TAKEAWAYS

★ **Physical Well-being and Leading by Example**: Prioritize physical health by exercising, eating well, and getting enough rest, setting an example for children about the importance of self-care.

★ **Emotional Well-being and Building Healthy Boundaries**: Take time to recharge emotionally and set boundaries, teaching children the value of self-care and emotional resilience.

★ **Benefits to Mothers:** Mothers who prioritize their well-being feel more energized, patient, and emotionally present, enhancing their ability to nurture their children.

★ **Benefits to Children:** Children learn the importance of self-care, emotional regulation, and respect for boundaries, fostering healthier habits and emotional intelligence.

★ When you prioritize self-care, you're not just benefiting yourself. Still, you're also teaching your children invaluable lessons about balance, self-compassion, and caring for one's mental and physical health. By investing in your own well-being, you can show up as a more present, patient, and engaged mother, and you create an environment where your children see self-care as an essential part of a fulfilling and healthy life.

REFLECTIVE QUESTIONS

★   How can I create time for self-care in my daily routine?

_____

_____

_____

_____

_____

_____

_____

★   Am I modeling healthy self-care for my child?

_____

_____

_____

_____

_____

_____

_____

_____

★ What steps can I take to ensure I am refreshed?

_____

_____

_____

_____

_____

_____

_____

_____

AFFIRMATIONS

Caring for myself allows me to care better for my child.

I deserve rest, nourishment, and peace as much as my child does.

Taking time for myself is an act of love for my family.

I honor my needs without guilt or apology.

Self-care replenishes my patience, energy, and joy.

I model healthy habits and balance for my child.

It is okay to ask for help when I need support.

I release perfection and embrace progress in my self-care.

Prioritizing my well-being strengthens our family bond.

I am worthy of love, rest, and kindness from myself.

I listen to my body, mind, and heart and respond with care.

I create space for my own growth and happiness every day.

Taking care of myself is a foundation for nurturing my child.

I replenish my energy so I can be fully present with my child.

Self-care is not selfish; it is essential for our family's well-being.

BIBLE VERSES

★   "Come to me, all you who are weary and burdened, and I will give you rest." Matthew 11:28 (NIV)

★   "But those who hope in the Lord will renew their strength. They will soar on wings like eagles; they will run and not grow weary; they will walk and not faint." Isaiah 40:31 (NIV)

★   "He refreshes my soul. He guides me along the right paths for his name's sake." Psalms 23:3 (NIV)

★   "Do you not know that your bodies are temples of the Holy Spirit, who is in you, whom you have received from God? You are not your own; you were bought at a price. Therefore, honor God with your bodies." 1 Corinthians 6:19-20 (NIV)

PRAYER

Heavenly Father,

Thank You for the incredible gift of motherhood and the blessings of my children. I know I am called to love, nurture, and care for them, but I also recognize that I need Your help in caring for me. Lord, help me to prioritize my physical, emotional, and spiritual well-being so I can be the best version of myself for my children.

Please give me the strength and wisdom to recognize when I need rest and to take the time to care for my body. Help me to make healthy choices that honor the body You've given me so that I can have the energy to fully engage with my children and provide them with the love and attention they need. Show me the importance of nourishing my body, mind, and soul, and remind me that caring for myself is not selfish but necessary for being a better mother.

I also ask for Your help in nurturing my emotional well-being. Teach me to set healthy boundaries, communicate my needs with love and clarity, and make space for activities that bring joy and peace. Help me recognize when I need to step back and recharge to be more present and patient with my children. Grant me the emotional resilience to face the challenges of motherhood with grace and calm.

I pray for Your guidance in my spiritual life. Help me to stay grounded in You, seeking Your strength and wisdom in every moment of my day. Let my relationship with You be a source of peace and comfort, and may I model the importance of faith and self-care to my children. Teach me how to balance my responsibilities as a mother with my need for spiritual renewal and connection.

Thank You, Lord, for the gift of motherhood and Your endless love and support. May I reflect Your grace as I care for my children and learn to care for myself so I can continue to be a loving, present, and joyful mom.

In Jesus' name, I pray. Amen.

CHAPTER 12

Nurture Your Child's Spiritual Growth

Between managing the household, working, and caring for my children's physical and emotional needs, I sometimes struggled to find the time or energy to focus on their spiritual development. I wanted them to grow strong in their faith, but I often felt like I was failing at growing mine. I felt like I was stretched too thin to be the spiritual leader for them. I was constantly juggling responsibilities, and while I was dedicated to ensuring they were healthy, happy, and well-adjusted, I sometimes felt like their spiritual growth took a backseat. I was also concerned I might not have the right words to guide them, or I worried that my own struggles with faith might influence theirs. There was also a sense of guilt, feeling like I should be doing more to help them connect with God, but in the busyness of life, it felt hard to prioritize it as often as I should.

When I felt defeated, I surrendered my fears and insecurities to Him and prayed, "Lord, help me trust that You are working in my child's heart, even when I feel like I'm not doing enough." I remind myself that I don't have to be perfect; God is with us in the journey. I found wisdom in scriptures like Proverbs 22:6, which promises that if I train my children how they should go, they will not depart from it. This reassured me that God is in control and my efforts, even when small, are part of His plan.

Instead of feeling defeated, I have learned to focus on small, intentional moments where I can model faith for my children through prayer before meals, talking about God's love in everyday situations, listening to praise and worship music while driving, and showing them how I lean on Him in times of struggle. I trust that God's grace covers my shortcomings, and I believe that even in the busyness and exhaustion, He will help me guide my children spiritually. By surrendering my doubts and relying on His strength, I am reminded that I am not alone in this, and God's love will be the foundation for their faith. These small actions, though seemingly simple, lay a strong foundation for their spiritual growth. Through them, I am teaching my children that faith is woven into the fabric of everyday life, not just something confined to church or formal prayer times.

Nurturing your children's spiritual growth is one of the most potent ways to equip them for life's challenges. A strong foundation of faith and values gives children a sense of purpose, hope, and moral direction to guide them throughout their lives. When they have a deep relationship with God, they can weather the storms of life with greater resilience. As a mother, encouraging your children's spiritual journey involves much more than simply teaching them about God; it means modeling a life of faith, engaging in spiritual practices together, and helping them understand the importance of a personal relationship with God. The way I live my faith, the choices I make, and the ways I model Christ's love to shape my children's view of God and His role in their lives. Through these practices, you instill a deep sense of purpose and resilience in your child that will serve them throughout their life.

Jesus also demonstrated the importance of spiritual growth, especially in children. In Matthew 19:14 (NIV), He said, "Let the little children come to me and do not hinder them, for the kingdom of heaven belongs to such as these." Jesus welcomed and valued children, recognizing their openness to faith. Mothers can follow His example by creating an environment where their children feel encouraged to grow in their relationship with God. This means praying with them, answering their spiritual questions, modeling Christ-centered lives, and guiding them to develop their faith. Just as Jesus disciples and nurtured His followers, parents are responsible for leading their children toward a lifelong journey with God.

By nurturing your children's spiritual growth, you help them develop a lasting foundation of faith that will guide them throughout their lives. Family devotions, prayer, and encouraging a personal relationship with God are powerful tools that can shape your child's character, values, and resilience. These moments, no matter how small, contribute to a lifetime of spiritual growth. As a mother, your influence in this area is profound, and by modeling faith in your own life, you create an environment where your child feels supported, loved, and inspired to pursue their spiritual journey.

Let's look at some examples of how nurturing your child's spiritual growth benefits mothers and children.

Family Devotions and Spiritual Connection:

Trina has two children, Von and Penelope, aged 8 and 10. Trina recognized early on that, to cultivate her children's faith, she needed to make spiritual practices a consistent part of their everyday lives. Rather than seeing prayer and Bible reading as isolated activities, Trina incorporated them into her family's routine.

Every evening, before bed, Trina and her children would gather for family devotions. They would read a short passage from the Bible, discuss its meaning, and pray together. At first, Von and Penelope were restless and sometimes didn't understand everything they read, but Trina was patient. She made the devotions interactive by asking them questions about the passage, allowing them to share their thoughts and feelings. She emphasized that prayer was a ritual and a personal conversation with God, encouraging her children to speak about their day, concerns, and gratitude.

Over time, Von and Penelope began to look forward to these moments. They found comfort in the prayers, joy in the stories, and strength in the lessons they learned. Trina noticed that her children were becoming more thoughtful about their actions and attitudes. They would often refer to lessons they had learned during their devotions when faced with challenges, like being kind to others or forgiving when someone hurt them. Through this consistent practice of family devotions, Trina nurtured her children's understanding of faith and strengthened their personal connection to God.

Teaching children God's way: Proverbs 22:6 NIV states "Start children off on the way they should go, and even when they are old, they will not turn from it." Trina's consistent practice of family devotions mirrors this principle, as she instills faith and biblical lessons in her children, helping them grow in wisdom and strengthen their personal relationship with God.

Encouraging a Personal Relationship with God:

Gina has a teenager, Kadijah, who has always participated in church activities. However, Gina noticed that Kadijah was beginning to view her faith more as a set of rules to follow rather than a personal relationship with God. Gina wanted to help Kadijah develop a deeper, more meaningful connection with God that was personal and not just based on external expectations.

Gina began having regular conversations with Kadijah about her faith, asking her questions like, "What does your relationship with God look like?" or "How do you feel God is speaking to you right now?" Gina encouraged Kadijah to pray independently and explore her spiritual questions without pressure from others' expectations. She also supported Kadijah in finding ways to express her faith outside a church, such as journaling, volunteering, or engaging in activities that brought her closer to God.

One day, Gina noticed a shift in Kadijah's perspective. She found Kadijah sitting in her room with her Bible open, praying quietly, something she hadn't seen her do before. Kadijah shared with her mom that she felt a deeper connection to God and wanted to develop her personal relationship with Him beyond church and family devotions. Gina was deeply moved by this, realizing she was helping her daughter build a personal and transformative faith by encouraging Kadijah to take ownership of her spiritual life.

By nurturing Kadijah's relationship with God this way, Gina taught her daughter the importance of cultivating an internal and relational faith, not just external and ritualistic. Gina's support helped Kadijah understand that faith is a journey that requires personal effort and that God is always there, inviting her to deepen that connection.

Seeking a Personal Relationship with God: Jeremiah 29:13 (NIV) reads "You will seek me and find me when you seek me with all your heart." Gina's nurturing of Kadijah's relationship with God encourages her to understand faith as a personal and relational journey, highlighting the importance of seeking God with sincerity and devotion, not just through external rituals.

KEY TAKEAWAYS

★   **Modeling Faith and Spiritual Practices:** A mother nurtures her child's spiritual growth by integrating prayer, Bible reading, and discussions about faith into daily life, demonstrating the importance of a personal relationship with God.

★   **Encouraging Personal Faith Ownership:** By creating space for children to explore their own spiritual questions and practices, a mother helps them develop a deeper, personal connection with God beyond rituals or expectations.

★   **Benefits for Mothers:** Sharing spiritual practices, fosters meaningful conversations and creates opportunities to grow together and faith, enhancing the parent–child relationship.

★   **Benefits to Children:** A foundation of faith gives the child a sense of purpose, hope, and strength to navigate life challenges with confidence and integrity.

REFLECTIVE QUESTIONS

★   How can I make spiritual practices a regular part of my child's life?

_____

_____

_____

_____

_____

_____

_____

★   Do I provide opportunities for my child to ask questions and grow in their faith?

_____

_____

_____

_____

_____

_____

_____

_____

★ Am I intentional in modeling a genuine relationship with God for my child to witness?

_____

_____

_____

_____

_____

_____

_____

_____

AFFIRMATIONS

I guide my child with faith, love, and wisdom.

I create opportunities for my child to explore their spiritual beliefs.

I model a life rooted in faith and integrity for my child to follow.

I encourage my child to seek God's guidance in all aspects of life.

I nurture my child's sense of gratitude and wonder every day.

I pray for my child's growth, protection, and purpose.

I teach my child to trust in God's plan for their life.

I help my child develop values that will guide their decisions and actions.

I celebrate my child's spiritual milestones, no matter how small.

I show my child the importance of kindness, compassion, and love.

I model honesty, patience, and forgiveness so my child can learn from my example.

I encourage my child to seek answers, ask questions, and grow in faith.

I provide a safe space for my child to express their spiritual journey.

I help my child see God's presence in everyday life.

I am committed to nurturing my child's spiritual, emotional, and moral growth.

BIBLE VERSES

★ "Start children off on the way they should go, and even when they are old, they will not turn from it." Proverbs 22:6 (NIV)

★ "I have no greater joy than to hear that my children are walking in the truth." 3 John 1:4 (NIV)

★ "But as for me and my household, we will serve the Lord." Joshua 24:15 (NIV)

PRAYER

Heavenly Father,

Thank You for the precious gift of my children. I am so grateful for the opportunity to guide them as they grow in faith and understanding of You. I am called to nurture their physical, emotional, and spiritual growth. Lord, I ask for Your wisdom and guidance as I help my children develop a strong foundation of faith and values that will serve them throughout their lives.

Please help me create an environment in our home where faith is nurtured daily. Give me the strength to prioritize family devotions, prayer, and conversations about You. Help me to make these moments meaningful and engaging so that my children understand the importance of a personal relationship with You. May our time together in Your Word strengthen their hearts and minds, and may they come to know You profoundly and personally.

I also pray that You give me the patience and grace to walk alongside my children in their spiritual journeys. As they encounter challenges and struggles, help me to guide them with love, compassion, and understanding. I pray that they come to know that their faith is not just about following rules but about building a relationship with You that will provide them with peace, joy, and guidance in every aspect of their lives.

I pray that my children grow up with hearts open to You, eager to seek Your will, and ready to trust in Your guidance. May they always know that You are with them, no matter where life takes them. Thank You for the privilege of being their mother. I trust that You are always working in their hearts and minds, shaping them into the people. You created them to be.

In Jesus' name, I pray. Amen.

CONCLUSION

Single parenting is a journey filled with joys, challenges, laughter, and tears. It's a role that demands your heart, energy, and faith, often testing you in ways you never expected. There will be days when the weight of it all feels heavy, and other days when the rewards are immeasurable. But through it all, you are shaping lives and impacting hearts in ways you may not fully realize in the moment. As you reflect on the principles and practices in this book, I hope you feel encouraged to embrace this journey with intention, humility, and love, knowing that each step you take as a parent is part of a greater purpose.

Every child is a unique masterpiece entrusted to us for a fleeting season. The days may sometimes feel long, but the years are undeniably short. Time passes quickly, and the precious moments we have with our children are fleeting. You can shape your child's life, character, values, and faith in this limited time. The extraordinary work of single parenting takes place in the ordinary moments, the bedtime stories, the shared meals, the small victories, and even the struggles. These moments may feel insignificant at the time, but they are the building blocks that form the foundation of your child's heart and soul. Don't underestimate the power of the simple, everyday actions that weave love, faith, and connection into your child's life.

Single parenting is not about perfection. You will make mistakes, and so will your child. There will be moments of missteps, frustrations, and things you wish you could do over. But gratefully, God's grace is sufficient to fill the gaps. His love covers our imperfections and gives us the strength to keep going. So, lean on Him in moments of doubt, and trust in His ability to guide you as you guide your child. Trust that even in your weakness, His power is made perfect. Remember, God does not call us to be flawless parents; He calls us to be faithful ones. He asks us to show up, to love deeply, to learn from our mistakes, and to trust that He is working through us to fulfill His purposes in our children's lives.

As you nurture your child's emotional, intellectual, and spiritual growth, don't forget to nurture yourself as well. A well-cared-for parent is better equipped to care for their child. Just as you prioritize your child's needs, it's essential to prioritize your own well-being emotionally, physically, and spiritually. Seek community with others on this journey, find moments to recharge, and stay rooted in prayer and Scripture. Single parenting is a marathon, not a sprint; it requires endurance, faith, and the ability to pace yourself. Your faith in God's provision and strength will sustain you through the toughest moments and renew your energy for the days ahead.

Lastly, celebrate the little victories. Every milestone, every act of kindness, every answered prayer is a testament to the love and effort you've poured into your role as a parent. These moments are often more significant than they appear on the surface. Whether it's your child's first word, a quiet moment of connection, or the way your child handles a difficult situation with grace these are the fruits of your labor. You are doing holy work, and your investment in your child will bear fruit for generations.

Thank you for allowing this book to be part of your parenting journey. May it serve as a reminder that you are not alone. God is with you, cheering you on, strengthening your heart, and equipping you for the beautiful, messy, and miraculous adventure of raising children.

NOTES

www.ingramcontent.com/pod-product-compliance
Lightning Source LLC
Chambersburg PA
CBHW051209120626
46547CB00013B/1279